All Their Splendour

David Alan Brown was born in 1922 and educated at Monkton Combe School, the London College of Divinity and the School of Oriental and African Studies, University of London. He has a distinguished academic background, including an MTh in Hebrew, Aramaic and Syriac, and a BA with First Class Honours in Classical Arabic.

He spent a great part of his working life as a missionary in the Sudan, and then had 'two marvellous years' (1963–65) studying the life of the Prophet Muhammad in Arabic with Muslim teachers in the Universities of Khartoum and Amman.

Returning to Britain in 1966 he served churches in the Diocese of Canterbury until in 1973 he became Bishop of Guildford.

He is also Chairman of the General Synod Board for Mission and Unity; the British Council of Churches Committee for Relations with People of Other Faiths; and the Conference of European Churches Islam in Europe Committee.

David Brown is the author of several books, amongst them *A Manual of Evangelism*, *The Way of the Prophet*, *A Catechism for Enquirers, Catechumens and Confirmation Candidates*, *Jesus and God*, *The Christian Scriptures*, *The Cross of the Messiah*, *The Divine Trinity*, etc.

DAVID BROWN

BISHOP OF GUILDFORD

All Their Splendour

World Faiths: A Way to Community

*With a Preface by
the Archbishop of Canterbury,
Dr Robert Runcie*

Collins

FOUNT PAPERBACKS

First published in 1982 by Fount Paperbacks, London

© David Brown, 1982

Set in 10 on 12pt Laser Plantin

Made and printed in Great Britain
by William Collins Sons & Co Ltd, Glasgow

Contents

Contents

Preface

The next generation will be surprised that we have paid so little attention in our theological writing to the questions raised by the increased contact between the great world religions.

Improved communications and decades of great human migration have already blurred the frontiers of the religious map of the world. In England, for example, it is becoming insensitive to draw up plans for religious education which ignore the presence of substantial communities of Muslims, Sikhs and Hindus. It is vital that we explore the creative possibilities of this new religious mixture.

The Bishop of Guildford has been a prophetic voice in this field, alerting fellow-Christians to the need to educate themselves about the divergencies and similarities between the major religious traditions. He is very well-equipped for this task, both academically and by reason of his distinguished service in the Sudan. In *All Their Splendour* he has attempted to discern the common themes running through all religious experiences which might enable the 'religions' to make a constructive contribution to the development of the world community. He has distilled many years of reflections on a subject which deserves to be taken very seriously. I hope his book will be widely read and studied.

March 1982   † Robert Cantuar

Author's Note

I have transliterated words in languages other than English as accurately as is necessary for clarity. It is impossible to achieve complete consistency but I have worked to the following principles.

Some well-known names and titles are used in their Anglicized forms without further accentuation, including Muhammad, Mecca, Islam, Upanishads, Vedas, Krishna, Nirvāna.

Arabic and Sanskrit words follow conventional practice in the reference books.

Buddhist terms are given in their Sanskrit, not Pāli, forms and in accordance with Christmas Humphreys' *A Popular Dictionary of Buddhism* (London, 1975).

Jewish words conform closely to the transliteration used in the Prayer Book of the Reform Synagogues.

In quotations, I have mainly followed the original author but not in all circumstances.

Introduction

This book takes seriously, but not uncritically, the claims of religions other than Christianity, to reveal truth about God and to bring their adherents into a life-sustaining relationship with him. It assumes that God is present always and everywhere as creator and redeemer, and that all his creatures experience, in one way or another, his grace. Its readers may well wish to ask how its author reconciles these assumptions and this recognition of religious experience which is not Christian with the affirmations which the churches make about Jesus Christ, and which he himself shares.

The churches declare that in the conception and birth of Jesus of Nazareth God entered into a new relationship with the created universe, that God revealed himself uniquely in the person and teaching of Jesus, and that in his passion and resurrection God gave humanity a new beginning. These claims have often been interpreted in such a way as to depreciate all religious experience and teaching which are not explicitly Christian; they appear to make an absolute distinction between the acts of God in Christ and his activity elsewhere in human history.

Interpreted in this exclusive way, the affirmation of Christ as God's word and man's saviour causes difficulties both for Christians who meet with people of other faiths and for those who wish to understand Christian beliefs sympathetically. But serious as the difficulties are, they should not deter Christians from joining in dialogue with others, or from exploring with them the themes, common to all religions, which have played so large a part in the formation of the human tradition.

Concern for others as fellow-subjects of God's royal rule is a prominent theme throughout the Bible; God's Spirit, active in creation and human achievement, is like the wind in blowing where it wills. In the New Testament, St Paul's sermon at Athens is given in the Acts of the Apostles as an example of the Christian message presented to educated Greeks; it took as its starting-point the universal relationship of God with the many races of mankind and expressed it in terms taken deliberately from Hellenistic philosophy. Moreover, the binding together of both Old and New Testaments in one Bible shows that Christians have from the first century onwards recognized the experience of Israel, set out in the Jewish scriptures, to be an authentic relationship with God. Throughout the history of the Church a notable series of scholars and others have recognized within other traditions echoes of truths and attitudes which are central to the Christian faith. They include the early apologists, particularly Justin Martyr and Clement of Alexandria, who wrestled with the status of Greek philosophy in the second century AD, and the two great missionaries of the sixteenth and seventeenth centuries, Matteo Ricci and Roberto de Nobili who sought to interpret the Gospel in ways which were congenial to the philosophies of China and of India. In our own times a growing number of Christian theologians have disclosed for others the presence of God within other traditions. The quality of this recognition is beautifully expressed in a study of the Muslim woman mystic Rābi'ah of Baṣra by Sister Mary Paul of the Sisters of the Love of God:

'Rābi'ah loved God for himself alone, and this, according to all the masters of the spiritual life, is the highest degree of love. In this love, which will be fully experienced only when the veil is raised in eternity, Muslims, Jews, Christians, and "all mankind to be saved" will be totally at one in Him who is blissful, limitless love.'

Christians recognize the religious experience of people who are adherents of other faiths as authentic, because they discern within it marks of the divine grace which is familiar to them through their faith in Jesus Christ. This does not mean an uncritical acceptance of all that other religions teach or practise. Many of their beliefs are contradictory to the Gospel, and some of their practices appear inconsistent with the principles of justice and peace. I do not wish to minimize these differences, any more than I wish to suggest that there is unanimity between the Christian churches or that their actions are always true to the Gospel which they proclaim. But I believe that at the heart of every religious community is an experience of relationship with the one living God which carries its own authentic hallmarks.

We live in a period of change which is radically different from all that have preceded it. Societies are no longer homogeneous; we know far more than previous generations about the practices of communities other than our own. The range of historical study has been greatly increased both in extent and in time by the work of archaeologists, and the perspectives of science have grown immeasurably. The way in which communities express their beliefs about the meaning of existence also reflects the circumstances and level of knowledge in which they originated; that which sufficed in earlier years will not suffice us now. They are all 'interim theologies' which need constant revision.

Introduction

Theologians should take account of the beliefs and practices of faiths other than their own, and revise both their assessment of history and also their doctrines of God's revelation in and to his creation. This revision has hardly begun. We must move from an emphasis upon the uniqueness of particular events and persons which excludes from consideration other manifestations of God's gracious presence, to an appreciation of those same events and persons as having universal significance for the whole life of mankind.

Many Christians hesitate to do this for fear lest they betray the unique position which the churches claim for Christ, and so make the coming of his kingdom more difficult. This is to misunderstand the implications of Christian belief; it was in his passion and death that Christ disclosed most completely the relationship between God and his creation. He revealed thereby the manner of his kingdom and the means by which it will be established. If this gentle, suffering and selfless man is the incarnation of the divine love, then his disciples are called to show a similar gentleness and moderation in the shared quest for world community. Christians are called to give, not to get, to nurture others rather than themselves, to place the advantage of others before their own. It is the way of Jesus himself which they are called to follow.

Christians are people of hope; they believe that God has a purpose in creation which will come to its fulfilment only when, to use St Paul's words, 'the whole universe is brought into a unity in Christ' (Ephesians 1. 10). But that hope does not diminish or depreciate the worth and splendour of the whole human achievement. Christ is incarnate within humanity and the Christian hope is that the many diverse enterprises of mankind will be enhanced by finding their own particular fulfilments within the harmonious integration of the whole universe in Christ. Before that hope can come, however, in its fulness, the human community must first be reconciled in a unity which does not destroy its many diversities, but which affirms them and transcends them.

In writing this book I have had direct access to the Bible and the Qur'ān, both of which I read in the original languages. I have used mainly the *Good News Bible*, except where indicated. I have translated the Qur'ān direct but with one eye on Dr Arberry's classic translation. I am entirely dependent on English translations of the Hindu, Buddhist and Chinese scriptures, and have used those versions which make the text clear in particular contexts.

My very grateful thanks are due to friends who have helped me in various ways including the Rev. Canon Colin Semper, the Rt Rev. David Young, Mr Bernard Nicholls, the Rev. Roger Hooker, and my colleague, the Rev. Kenneth Cracknell. None of them bears any responsibility for what I have written. Mrs Joan Simpson has typed successive drafts of the text with patience, accuracy and care. My wife Mary has helped me in all manner of ways, and not least by her constant encouragement.

DAVID BROWN

CHAPTER I

Towards Tomorrow

1. *Community*

Among the many scientific and technological advances of
our time, perhaps the most important has been the enor-
mous advance in communications. Radio and television
have created world audiences for royal weddings and
funerals, for football matches and for presidential and
papal installations; news is instantly shared by people all
over the world. Even now we are only on the threshold
of developments made possible by the use of micro-
processors and satellites. New methods of communication
are matched by the greatly increased speed of travel; super-
sonic aeroplanes have made our planet 'a twelve-hour
world'.

These changes affect our lives in two ways. First, they
offer to ordinary people a wider range of options from
which to construct their own particular understanding of
the world and their part in it. In earlier generations people
'knew where they were'; they shared with their neighbours
a framework of reference, religious, social and political,
by which to interpret almost everything that happened to
them and their families. Most people knew very little about
the ways in which other nations lived or the beliefs they
held. That is no longer the case. Television documentaries
which give the background to the news – Iran's Islamic
revolution, African politics, Japanese business methods or
the exploration of space, and informative serials raise

questions in our minds about the nature and destiny of man, and about religion. In schools, colleges and universities, young people are introduced to a variety of systems of belief and social organization, and to different ways of life and behaviour. As a consequence, we are more aware than our predecessors were of other religions, philosophies and ideologies, and of their worth. We have discovered also that our traditional religion or understanding of the world does not of itself have all the answers to the questions which must now be asked about the universe and mankind's place within it.

Secondly, many nations and communities which in the past were largely homogeneous now contain large groups of people who come from different ethnic origins, who follow different cultural patterns, or who practise religions different from those of the majority. This has happened in western Europe for all kinds of reasons: the recruitment of migrant labour for particular industries, the obligations incurred through earlier efforts to colonize Asia and Africa, the attraction of the developed social services of the host countries. Britain, it is true, has in the past absorbed many different ethnic groups who came to her shores from Europe for conquest or for refuge, but since the Second World War she has become pluralist in a new way with the immigration of people from the West Indies, East Africa, India and Pakistan. There are nearly one million Muslims living in Britain, as well as many Sikhs, Hindus and Buddhists and although those of West Indian origin are mostly Christians, many belong to churches and groups which are markedly different from the mainstream churches.

The problems associated with pluralism are not new, and they have existed ever since the first cities drew together people from different clans, with a variety of skills, to support communities which transcend the ties of blood and kinship. In the Middle and Near East, the so-called heartlands of Islam, there have always been large Christian minorities – the Copts in Egypt number more than three million people – and in the Indian sub-continent Hindus and Muslims, as well as Buddhists, Sikhs, Christians and others, have lived together for centuries. Even after the creation of the Muslim states of Pakistan and Bangladesh, there were nearly fifty million Muslims still living in India. In other parts of Asia, including China and Japan, there has always been religious pluralism, and Buddhism in particular has been practised alongside and together with traditional religions. In AD 1453 the Turks captured Constantinople, and Islam spread into eastern Europe where large Muslim groups now live alongside the Christian majority, particularly in Yugoslavia and Bulgaria. There are some twenty million Muslims in the southern parts of the Soviet Union. In Africa also, particularly in the Sudan belt which runs across the continent south of the Sahara, both Islam and, more recently, Christianity have won converts from those who have hitherto followed traditional religions. Some of these countries have Muslim majorities, others Christian, but in almost all of them Christians and Muslims work side by side in the building of their new nations: in some areas to be Muslim or Christian is a matter for personal choice and no longer of national or tribal significance. Many of the larger islands, in the Pacific and off the African coast, have mixed communities in which several different religions are practised.

The existence of different racial, cultural or religious groups within one society and the question whether they can live together with mutual tolerance and understanding are not new problems. They have been faced and solved, in different ways, all through history, in many different areas of the world. Several factors, however, associated with the circumstances of the twentieth century can make the problems of pluralism particularly acute.

In earlier ages, migration was a slow and costly process which allowed time for adjustment and assimilation; today journeys take hours rather than months. The expectations of modern democratic societies also contribute to the heightening of tension in societies which have recently taken in large numbers of immigrants; the longstanding members of such societies find it difficult to concede the developed rights and privileges of, for instance, social welfare to those who have suddenly become their fellow-citizens. This is especially so in areas of deprivation or poverty where such rights are only exercised with difficulty, even by the majority group.

If pluralist societies today are to be united and harmonious, time and space are needed for immigrants to be absorbed by the host community at a moderate pace, governments must act with fairness and justice and be seen as stable sources of authority to which all the diverse interests in a country can look for protection and support, the structure and services of society must operate for the benefit of all without discrimination, and the processes of law must be applied in an even-handed way. Every group must be free to participate in the life of the whole society and on equal terms with others: to contribute to its development and to share in its wealth and prosperity. Every group must also be ready to adjust to achieve the well-being of the society of which it is a part.

In this century we cannot aim for anything but a pluralist

community in which people of all races, of all cultures, of all religions share a common life together. This unification, however, must be one which allows every particular country, or large group, to make its own particular contribution to the life of the whole. 'The new contract which the South seeks with the North, the poor with the rich – rests firmly and securely on the premise that the dependent relationships of the past have served the world badly; that isolation is not an option open to even the most powerful countries; that a world order dominated by concepts of sovereignty and founded on an adversary system is irrelevant and inimical to contemporary human needs and must be dismantled; that interdependence is the only valid basis for a human strategy of survival.' (1) These are the words of the Commonwealth Secretary-General, Shridath Ramphal, and Martin Luther King summed up what our aim must be: 'Every nation must develop an over-riding loyalty to mankind as a whole in order to preserve the best in their individual societies.' (2) The only unity which will serve mankind in its complexity and diversity, whether on the national or the international level, is one which takes seriously the plurality of ethnic groups, cultures, philosophies and religions which make up the human community, and enables each one to play its particular part in the common life.

Lewis Mumford gives a parable of this unity-in-diversity in the final chapter of *The City in History*. 'The electric power grid is a network of power plants, some big, some small, some worked by waterpower, some by coal, scattered over a large area, often thousands of square miles. Some of these plants by themselves could supply only their immediate community, others have greater range. Each unit in this system has a certain degree of self-sufficiency and self-direction, equal to ordinary occasions. But by being linked together, the power stations form a whole system whose parts, though relatively independent, can upon demand work as a whole, and make good what is lacking in any particular area. The demand may be made at any point in the system, and the system as a whole may be drawn on to respond to it. Though the whole is at the disposal of the part, it is the local user who determines when it shall be used and how much shall be taken. No single central power station, however big, would have the efficiency, the flexibility or the security of the whole grid, nor would it be capable of further growth, except by following the pattern of the grid.' (3) This seems to me a powerful parable in which to express the ideal of a pluralist society, in which each particular group plays a full part in the life of the whole community. For it is only as each group is allowed to contribute from its own resources to the well-being of the whole, that its members will feel secure, and able to accept the contributions of others. Yet each group must also be affected by the wider community in which they participate with others.

2. *Religion*

Pluralism creates problems at every level of community life, and not least for religious people. In some ways this is surprising since God, we may suppose, is concerned with the whole life of the universe in all its many different facets. He is the living Reality who is always there, relevant and contemporary in every different situation, but transcending it also, both in his being and sovereignty. Men pray to God and, at the same time, are conscious of his unfathomable riches and overwhelming power, like that of the ocean, whose waters we can touch and use, but which stretches, aloof and mysterious, beyond the horizon. The witness of the different religions is unanimous in this, for not one would claim an exhaustive knowledge of God as he is in himself. He is the infinite and eternal, whose nature and being a thousand names cannot adequately express.

Contemporary life-styles in western Europe are largely secularist in attitude, with an emphasis upon material goods and values. Many of the world's peoples profess Marxist creeds which deny any reality beyond the natural universe. Yet even in Marxist states people persist in their beliefs; Christians and Muslims continue to profess and to practise their religion, despite the difficulties, in Russia and eastern Europe. (4) In China there has been a revival of Taoist philosophy and the practice of religion is now permitted by the government. Religion does not diminish human nature but enhances it, even at the heights of scientific and technological achievement.

Religion has often failed its adherents and through the centuries religious controversy has caused much suffering. In the history of every religion there have been periods when its practice has served false, even vicious, ends; there have been areas where belief has become superstition, and loyalty stagnation or an excuse for oppression. Nevertheless, it is also true that religious experience has made significant contributions to the intellectual, moral and spiritual development of mankind. Human existence has been immensely enriched by religious beliefs and ideals and by the varied practices of worship. Through their liturgies and through reflection upon the mysteries lying beyond their own competence, men and women have discovered a meaningful coherence in the universe of which they are part. They have also discovered new horizons challenging them to reach out beyond their own environments and to explore distant and unknown territory. I do not wish to argue here for the reality of religious experience since the following chapters are themselves testimony to the fact that on the widest scale of observation possible human people have found it to be genuine; I believe also that, despite the many questions which may be asked about religious formulations and statements about man's place in the universe and his destiny, religious experience will continue to play an important part in the development of mankind. The basic question which underlies so many of our contemporary problems is how to bring people to fulfilment as beings who are developed, mature and wise enough to be able to cope with the greatly extended opportunities and responsibilities which are available to many who are alive today. (5) History suggests that religion must play a part in finding an answer to that question, as it has in the past.

Can religion, however, have a place in the pluralist world of our times, either within particular countries or regions, or in relation to the world community of tomorrow? Or will the traditionally conservative and exclusive attitudes associated with religions prevent them from making a contribution to the building of open and harmonious plural societies?

The problems and opportunities of pluralist communities, whether on the world scene or within particular countries, face believers as much as they do others. Believers must learn, like everyone else, to work in harmony with people who belong to different ethnic groups or cultures, and to live at peace with those who practise a faith different from their own. For most people who profess a religion, this is a new experience. Christianity grew out of Judaism, and Islam developed within an environment in which both Christianity and Judaism had some influence; Buddhism grew out of Hinduism. But for the greater part of their history, these religions have mainly been practised within environments where they have been the dominant, if not the only, religious faith. Even in India or the Middle East, for instance, where there were communities of different faiths within one country, one of the faiths usually dominated; members of others were in a minority. Adherents of different faiths rarely met as equals. Christendom was identified with western Europe and the Americas, which were religiously homogeneous, and, despite the presence of Christian minorities, the Near and Middle East were, in Islamic terms, *Dār al-Islām*, the Area of Islam, and traditionally set over against *Dā'r al-Ḥarb*, the Area of War, i.e. that of the non-Muslim peoples. Many areas of the world, China and large parts of Asia and the Indian sub-continent for instance, were isolated from contact with other countries, and their religions and teachings developed in ignorance of the ideas and values of others.

Isolation and cultural dominance, however, have not been the only factors to hinder religious communities from responding positively to the beliefs and teachings of others. The awareness of God's presence which lies at the heart of religious experience is always mediated to the worshipper in a particular way and through particular means of grace which are then endowed with special and unique significance. A Muslim, for example, identifies the Qur'ān with the actual word of God and believes that Muhammad was the 'Seal of the prophets' through whom God gave his Word to mankind in a final and definitive way. He cannot, therefore, easily accept the genuineness of any religious experience which does not conform to the teaching of the Qur'ān or recognize the authority of Muhammad. A Christian believes that God intervened in history in a unique and personal way through his Son Jesus Christ, and he finds it difficult to accept any religious experience which makes no acknowledgement of the unique ministry of Jesus. A Buddhist believes that the Buddha taught the one way by which a person may achieve the salvation identified with *Nirvāna*, 'the place of bliss' beyond the phenomena and suffering of earthly existence; there are for him no other ways so effective by which to achieve that end. Hinduism, which embraces a great variety of different cults and philosophies, appears more tolerant, but Hindus often identify Hinduism with Indian nationalism and are antagonistic towards the exclusive claims which Muslims or Christians make for the particular revelations which they claim to have been given by God.

Associated with the exclusive claims which religions make for their own beliefs is the missionary activity which seeks to win converts from the adherents of other faiths. Missionary activity has been a feature of all the major religions except Hinduism from their foundation. Buddhist missionaries were sent out by the Indian emperor, Aśoka, as early as the third century BC, and in later centuries Buddhism was carried into China, Korea and Japan; Buddhism continues to win converts and there are Buddhist centres for spreading the faith in many European countries. Islam has always been a missionary religion, not only in the Near and Middle East, but also in Africa, and since AD 1400 in south-east Asia through the efforts of Muslim traders and teachers and more recently of Muslim rulers. In recent years Islamic Cultural Centres have also been established in many major cities of western Europe and North America. These missionary activities reflect in part the political and economic nationalism of the age through which the human community is still passing and are appropriate to it. But their deepest motivation is the obligation to share the faith, an essential characteristic of all religions which make universal claims. Truth is of universal significance and it must always remain a duty for those who have grasped it, or have been grasped by it, to share their insights with others. (I for one cannot evade the obligation to bear witness to Jesus Christ as Saviour and Lord.)

The communities of the different world faiths, however, are changing in ways which will enable them to make a more positive contribution to the growth of harmonious plural societies; their membership is ever more international. There are Buddhists now in most parts of the world besides the traditionally Buddhist areas of Asia, and large numbers of Muslims in Europe and America. Christianity also is an international religion with over one thousand million members drawn from most of the nations of the world. Its growth during the last hundred years has been particularly dramatic in Africa, and, although only a small proportion in the total population of the larger countries of Asia are Christians, there are significant Christian churches in them also. At the beginning of the present century only fifteen per cent of all Christians came from the Third World (Asia, Africa, Oceania and South America), but at its close, in AD 2000, it is estimated that Third World Christians will be in the majority. (6)

The greatly increased mobility of people and ideas is also changing the composition of the communities of the major faiths. No longer are they dominated by people from one particular area of the world, Christianity by Europeans and North Americans and Islam by the Arabs: their memberships are becoming more diverse and made up of many different races, cultures and backgrounds. They are becoming universal communities, in which diversities of language, custom, philosophy and commitment will be accepted as an enrichment and a source of strength.

The development of modern science, with its secular ways of thinking, is also changing the world faiths. In Christianity, which responded first to the challenge of modern science, this produced a new attitude to the scriptures and a more reflective and intuitive understanding of Christian doctrines. In contrast with the Christian experience, however, Islamic theology is only now beginning to come to terms with scientific theories which challenge the status and authority of the Qur'ān, the traditional cosmology of Islamic theology, and the provisions of the religious law. It is too early to predict what will happen to Islamic theology which at the moment remains, for the most part, in the hands of conservative scholars. Buddhism also, although it often appears attractive with its emphasis on self-discipline and knowledge of the self, has not yet fully faced the insights of modern psychology and medicine or the questions which may be asked of it in the light of our knowledge of the processes of evolution.

The several religions record in their different ways how peoples have, in particular environments and circumstances, expressed their awareness of the presence of the Transcendent, and of the relationship which they believe they have had with it. They are testimonies to what they have heard of the divine word, and expressions of the communion they have discovered in prayer. It is not possible, however, as yet to fit these testimonies and affirmations into one single system of theology. God transcends the most developed imagination of him and it is unreasonable to expect the different religions, coming from such diverse roots, to present a coherent theological map of God's long-standing relationships with humanity.

The basic patterns of that relationship, however, the word and the way, communion and healing, recur in almost all religions. Though expressed in different ways, the correspondence of ideas between them is sufficient to make their different theologies mutually intelligible and to provide bridges which those of the separate faiths may cross to share with one another their insights and their treasures. In the dialogue between them, they have both the opportunity and the means to make a valuable contribution to the building of world community.

3. *Dialogue*

It is not an easy task to develop contacts between members of different religions. Believers are often ignorant about other faiths; those who participate in formal inter-faith consultations and committees are often naïve in their expectations, even some highly placed politicians and religious dignitaries. There is also the normal innate fear of change and of the often imaginary threats posed by those who are different. But there are many benefits, and the opportunity which dialogue of this kind offers for religions to play a harmonizing role in the pluralist world of the future is expressed in words written by a participant at the Ajaltoun Consultation on Dialogue between Men of Living Faiths held in 1970.

'The dialogue is a sign of hope, both for the inside and the outside of man. By the very fact that we lived together, shared our common religious concern, and also prayed together, we were made to feel something new, something which cannot be put into words except that we were all too small before God, too small to dispute him among ourselves, and that we had just to surrender, kneel down, and pray ... To most of us the "other" faith was, before we actually met, an abstraction or just a different faith about which we knew less or more. But as we met, we became aware of a new situation, a kind of personal encounter, unfolding between us and within our common humanity which was, to translate it into religious terms, our common need of God.' (7)

Dialogue as it is practised, rather self-consciously, by the churches and other religious communities, represents, however, only a fragment of the 'dialogue' which now takes place all across the world wherever people of different faiths meet together in the everyday circumstances of community life. Although these meetings are not always held without antagonism or misunderstanding, or take place in political situations where one religious group is in a position to dominate others, or has a privileged position within the traditional culture or the educational system, there are many opportunities for believers of different faiths to meet on more open and equal terms. People who share a common citizenship, who are united in pursuit of a common goal, whether in a business or in the development of a nation, whose children go to the same schools, and who pay the same taxes, are more likely to share with each other the insights of their different faiths. In doing so they often discover how much they share in common as well as gain a clearer idea of the differences which remain between them. Many of the questions too which are raised by the network of international communications are about the relationships between the different religions and philosophies.

Much has been done during recent years to encourage dialogue between representatives of different religions at an institutional level. Both the World Council of Churches and the Vatican have been involved in this, and in Britain the British Council of Churches has recently issued *Guidelines* for the churches on this aspect of community relations. (8)

To join in dialogue with people of other faiths, at the corporate or the personal level, is a new experience for most people, and calls into question the exclusive claims of particular religions to teach the truth about God and human destiny. To participate in it successfully calls for willingness to listen to others and for more open attitudes towards their beliefs. The building of a harmonious world community will only be achieved if the religions of mankind are reconciled in a harmony which transcends them all.

To achieve this reconciliation is not so difficult as might be imagined. Those who do exchange ideas with people of other faiths are often surprised to discover that they echo their own religious experience at a variety of different levels. I do not mean that there is any general correspondence between the central beliefs of Christianity and Islam, or Islam and Buddhism, but simply that all religions contain concepts that are mutually intelligible and that at certain points the correspondence is more marked than at others. There are, for example, similarities between the practice of meditation as taught in Christianity, Islam and some forms of Buddhism, and between the ethical ideals of the different religious ways, the *Torah*, the *Sharī'a* and the Buddhist *Dharma*. At a recent Muslim-Christian consultation, a Muslim who had been pressing the claims of Islam upon me suddenly said: 'For me it is all summed up in the story of the Good Samaritan.' Buddhism reflects much of the Hindu philosophy from which it sprang, and Christianity and Islam share beliefs in the creation of the universe by God, the constant ordering of it by his will and providence, the revelation of his will to men by prophets and scripture, the resurrection and the last judgement.

While there are many correspondences at the conceptual and ethical levels, and in religious practices, it is often at the personal level that the individual believer finds kinship with those of another faith. Thus I recall with gratitude my long friendship with an Azharī doctor of divinity who has said his regular prayers in our home, an enchanted evening with a group of young Ṣūfīs in the Gazīrah who shared with me readings both from the New Testament and the Qur'ān, visits to the leaders of Muslim ṭarā'iq or religious brotherhoods, and a visit to a lonely mountain mosque in Palestine guarded by an old man whose grandfather and father, like Samuel of old, had given their lives to its rebuilding and maintenance. I sensed in each of them the reality of a God-ward sensitivity which I covet for myself. To share in people's joys and sorrows, at birth, marriage and in sickness or bereavement, is to share in a common humanity which lives in the presence of the One who is Father to us all. The correspondence between religions is grounded in two shared realities: the presence of God and the common humanity in which we are all kin to each other.

NOTES

1. Quoted in 'Commonwealth', December 1977.
2. Martin Luther King, *Chaos or Community?*, Penguin, 1969, 181.
3. Lewis Mumford, *The City in History*, Penguin, 1961, 643.
4. See e.g. Trevor Beeson, *Discretion and Valour*, Collins, 1974; revised edition Fount Paperbacks, 1982.
5. Cf. A. H. Maslow, *The Farther Reaches of Human Nature*, Penguin Books, 1976, 18–19.
6. See W. Buhlmann, *The Coming of the Third Church*, St Paul Publications, Slough, 1974, 20 and 130. For a sober estimate of the Christian Church's influence in Asia see *The Report of the Lambeth Conference, 1978*, London, 87–92.
7. The process is documented in *Christians Meeting Muslims*, World Council of Churches, 1977: S. J. Samartha, *Courage for Dialogue*, WCC, 1981: also publications of the Secretariat for Non-Christians.
8. *Christians Meeting Muslims*, 79–80.

CHAPTER 2

The Transcendent

At the heart of all religious experience is awareness of the transcendent, the recognition of something or someone, greater than all other objects in the natural universe, in whose presence man lives and to whom he has obligation. This basic theme underlies all the many different ways in which human beings have defined their relationships with the transcendent. At one end of the spectrum are the personal relationships between God and man affirmed in the three monotheisms, Judaism, Christianity and Islam, and at the other the largely impersonal concepts of *Dharma* (Truth) and *Tao* (Way) which make religious claims upon the lives of Buddhists and Taoists. We see this awareness at its simplest in the so-called traditional religions. But awareness of the transcendent, the presence of another reality worthy of worship, is not confined to believers alone. This awareness can be experienced, for example, listening to great music, or contemplating beauty in nature or in works of art, or in the intensity of deep and joyous personal relationships. Time stands still and a door is opened upon another dimension of existence more intense and more universal than the limitations of space and time would normally allow.

1. *The Primal Vision*

What are called the 'traditional religions' developed largely within isolated communities in which traditions embodying

31

the community's beliefs and rituals are handed on from one generation to another by word of mouth. Through them people, living in situations of poverty and simplicity, remote from any formal education or developed economy, express their response to the transcendent. These religions are not usually practised outside the communities in which they originated and even in them their influence has been much weakened by the advent of more universal religions, particularly Christianity and Islam. Nevertheless they have an integrity of their own and they illustrate basic elements in the religious experience of mankind. It is not, however, an easy task to describe them since they are related very intimately to the particular environments in which they are practised. I have, therefore, avoided wide generalization and chosen instead to present short descriptions of the beliefs and practices of people with most of whom I have had some personal contact.

The Nuer of the Sudan are a Nilotic people, inhabiting the swamp region on either side of the White Nile, and they follow a simple way of life based on the care of their herds of cattle and a rudimentary pattern of agriculture. (1) Yet, despite the absence of formal education or literature of any kind, they have developed a religion which not only gives coherence to their experience of life but also sustains and enriches it.

At the heart of Nuer religion is the recognition of spirit as that which is present throughout the world, determining all that happens. Spirit is associated particularly with the sky, but not identified with it; like wind and air, God, Spirit in the heavens, is the creator and mover of all things. He is in the sky, falls in rain, shines in the sun and moon, and blows in the wind. Other spirits, both of the sky and of the earth, are associated with 'Spirit in the sky', but not as beings distinct from each other. Spirit, in its various forms and manifestations, is the ever present mystery behind experience, with which the Nuer believe themselves to be in relationship.

God, 'Spirit in the sky', is the father of men, their protector and friend, the one who comforts and carries them as parents do their helpless infants. The Nuer feel themselves to be dependent upon Spirit, and speak of themselves as simple people who must acquiesce in what Spirit does to them. 'God is present' is a phrase they use especially when they wish to indicate that they do not know what to do but that God is with them and will help them. Yet although Spirit is felt to be present to them in the here and now, participating in the affairs of men, he is also felt to be far away in the sky. Thus Nuer attitudes towards Spirit range from love to fear, from trust to apprehension, from dependence to hostility.

The Nuer believe that they may communicate with 'Spirit in the sky' through prayer and sacrifices. Their prayers are most commonly made on public and formal occasions of either family or tribal significance. The Nuer make long invocations concerning the event or circumstance for which they pray; they introduce into these rambling addresses short prayers of petition, the following for example: 'Our father, it is your universe, it is your will, let us be at peace, let the souls of the people be cool, you are our father, remove all evil from our path.' Each petition may be used separately and not only as part of the invocations, but also in private and spontaneous prayer, whether spoken or inward, and as pious ejaculations. If he is in any trouble or anxiety, the head of a Nuer household will pace up and down his homestead brandishing his spear and uttering these supplications; or, less formally, he may say them, standing or squatting, with his eyes turned towards heaven and his arms outstretched from the elbows, moving his hands, palms uppermost, up and down. They may also be uttered in the petition a man on a journey makes to God to ensure success in the enterprise for which the journey is made.

The Nuer pray for deliverance from evil in a variety of images which express the ideal life as they imagine it to be: sleep, lightness, ease, coolness, softness, the steady fire burning in the homestead, abundant life, a clear path, tender pasture for the young animals.

The Nuer have few ritual prohibitions; what they fear is not ritual impurity, but the moral impurity or sin which leads to sickness or other misfortune. Thus, in sacrifice, it is not the outward physical state of the sacrificer which is important, but his moral state and the sincerity of his intention. The sense of dependence upon God which dominates Nuer religion is intimate and personal. Its emphasis is on complete surrender to God's will. (2)

Each of the traditional religions, like that of the Nuer, is unique and has particular features which reflect the circumstances in which its people live. There are, for example, differences in the ways in which they describe relationships between the supreme being, or high God, creator and father, and the many other spirits and deities associated with him. (3) In the words of Chief Ramon of the Digger Indians in California, 'in the beginning God gave to every people a cup of clay, and from this cup they drank their life. They all dipped in the water but their cups were different.' (4)

Despite the many differences, however, there is a remarkable continuity between the traditional religions. Writing of the African religions, John Taylor described them as sharing in what he calls 'a primal vision' of the divine presence. 'I find it impossible to dispute a universal recognition of, and desire for, the ultimate God. The proof for this seems to lie not so much in the titles of the creator which are used today in every tribe, for these may reflect an important teaching, but rather in the references everywhere in songs and proverbs and riddles, whose archaic grammatical forms attest their antiquity. These reveal the deep sense of a pervading presence – "The cattle shelter under the same tree with God." "Wherever the elands graze in herds, there is God." "God is in the great trunk and in the low branches." "If you would tell God, tell it to the wind." "God is in front: he is in the back." His praise-names, rather than the actual proper names now used, often reveal the same concept – "He who is met everywhere"; "Ocean with horizon headband"; "Infinity of the forest"; "He who fills all"; and the ancient farewell greetings "Go with God": "Stay with God".' (5)

We also have Pope Paul VI's message *Africae Terrarum*. 'A common and very important element of this spiritual conception is the idea of God as first and last cause of all things. This concept, which is felt rather than analysed, practised rather than pondered, is expressed in a manner that varies quite considerably according to the cultures. In reality the presence of God pervades traditional African life as the presence of a being who is superior, personal and mysterious. One turns to him at the solemn hours of life, and at its most critical moments. Almost always, once fear of his mighty power has been overcome, God is called on as father. The prayers addressed to him, individual or collective, are spontaneous and sometimes moving, while among the forms of sacrifice the outstanding one for purity of significance is that of the offering of the first fruits.' (6)

The 'traditional religions' help us to understand the important part which religion has always played in the development of human life as we now know it. To be aware of the divine presence, to recognize his transcendence and yet to call upon Spirit as father and protector, to pray and to petition, to offer gifts in sacrifice and to take care to offer them purely, to fear evil and its consequences, are deep human instincts which we all share. Although in particular cases their expression has been overlaid by superstition and oppressive social practices, they are the basic materials from which much of developed religious practice and belief has been built.

2. *On the Shore of the Ocean*

Human existence is very uneven in its happiness and fulfilment; some are born to wealth and well-being, free to lead interesting and active lives, while others are condemned from birth to poverty, to deprivation or to ill-health. Family fortunes also change and a family which is rich in one generation may be beggars in the next. Epidemics and disease, flood, drought and famine make life uncertain. At the national level also there is constant change, as now one faction, now another comes to power, or this or that country for a time dominates its neighbours. Is it possible to discern beneath the changing patterns of human existence progress towards any goal or transcendent purpose which would give it coherence? What element of stability can we discern in the world as we know it?

The answer of philosophical Hinduism is that we find neither stability nor truth if we search for them in the transient phenomena of our everyday lives. Instead we must search for them within ourselves, in the relationship between the real self at the ground of our being and the absolute which is the ground of all that exists in the whole universe and is itself the universal soul. (7) The transcendent is not wholly other, distinct from men, but kin with the essential element in each individual soul. To understand the relationship between the two is the aim of religion, and religious practices are directed towards its enhancement.

In contrast with the biblical notion of time as a process which began with creation and continues until the last judgement, Hindus believe that the universe passes through a continually recurring cycle of growth and dissolution, and the individual human soul through a succession of different existences. *Saṁsāra*, 'course' or 'revolution', is the Sanskrit word for these ever recurring cycles of change. 'For the Hindus the world was not created once for all nor was there any end to it: from all eternity it had been recreating itself and dissolving back into its unformed and "unmanifest" condition, and these periods of evolution and devolution were called days and nights of Brahmā. Each day and each night of Brahmā lasts one thousand years of the gods, and each year of the gods corresponds to twelve thousand years of men. Thus every day of Brahmā which sees the emanation of the universe from the divine substance and its dissolution back into it lasts twelve million years, and for twelve million more – the night of Brahmā – all remains absorbed in the One Brahman in a state of pure potentiality waiting to be once more actualized ... The world on each renewal emerges from the womb of Brahman perfect.' But it does not last, 'and theft, falsehood, and fraud creep in ... Such is the Hindu concept of the cosmos – beginningless and endless in time as well as in space – and the soul of man must ever anew embark on

37

this journey that has no end, passing from one life and from one body into another like a caterpillar moving on interminably from one blade of grass to the next ... From the smallest insect to the mightiest god the whole world is in a perpetual state of suppuration and decay. Oceans dry up and mountains topple down: all things are vanity, and only man is fool enough to desire them. He thirsts for life and the fulness of it, not knowing that it is this very love of life that keeps him a bondslave to the twin evils of *karma* and *saṁsāra – saṁsāra* that is like a well without water and man the frog that helplessly struggles in it.' (8)

In the philosophical system karma is simply the law of being in which every action has its appropriate result. Linked with the doctrine of the transmigration of souls, or reincarnation within successive existences of saṁsāra, this doctrine of karma became central within Hinduism. 'Those whose conduct on earth has given pleasure, can hope to enter a pleasant womb, that is, the womb of a Brāhmin, or a woman of the princely class, or a woman of the peasant class; but those whose conduct on earth has been foul can expect to enter a foul and stinking womb, that is, the womb of a bitch or a pig or an outcaste. But those small and continually returning creatures [like flies and worms] are not to be found on either of these two paths: [theirs is] a third condition, [for of them it is said:] "Be born and die".' (9)

The human soul, however, in its true essence is intimately related to Brahman, the unchanging and eternal Being which lies outside of space and time but is also the source of the transient and changing world of saṁsāra. The essential quest of religion, therefore, is 'to realize this eternal soul and to disengage it from its real or imaginary connection with the psychosomatic complex (i.e. the

individual human being), that thinks, wills and acts.' (10)
To achieve that end is to achieve *mokṣa*, liberation: it is
to be freed from the endless succession of earthly existences
(saṁsāra) and to enjoy integration with the one, unchanging Brahman. 'Mokṣa means "liberation, freedom, re-
lease". As a snake is "released" from its old skin, so is
the arrow of the *Ātman* [i.e. the essential eternal soul of
each human being] released . . . into the target of Brahman:
it is freedom to range at will as a bird flies through the
unobstructed air or as a fish swims through the boundless
ocean: it is freedom from the body and the trammels of
space and time which fetter the body, freedom to laugh
and play in the infinite.' (11)

The relationship between Brahman and ātman, the inner
self at the centre of every human person, is the one theme
which is central to the *Upanishads*. These treatises form
the bulk of the Hindu canonical scriptures, the four *Vedas*,
and are commentaries upon its other sections. (12) Since
they were written over a considerable period of time by
different authors, they explore the Brahman-ātman
relationship from many different points of view. In some
passages Brahman has the appearance of a personal god,
being the cosmic, universal soul (ātman), but in others is
described as an impersonal Absolute: Brahman is described
both as the lord and king of all beings, but also as the
timeless self in whom all beings exist. Thus there developed
within Hinduism several contrasting descriptions of mokṣa
or salvation. One tendency was towards monism; complete
identity between the liberated soul of man, and the Absolute; there is but one Brahman-ātman, which is Absolute
Being, Consciousness and Bliss. Another tendency was to
emphasize the correspondence of the human soul with
Brahman, the universal, cosmic soul, and their *relationship*

with each other. In contrast with them both, *Sāmkhya* teaching denied the union of the individual soul with Brahman. In this system mokṣa means the isolation of the individual soul from all other souls and the whole domain of nature; it does not mean union with Brahman but *liberation* into a perfect self-sufficiency like the timeless self-unity of the Absolute. (13)

According to the teaching of the Upanishads, salvation comes by way of true knowledge of the Brahman-ātman relationship, supported by ethical conduct.

> By knowing God there is a falling off of all fetters;
> With distresses destroyed, there is cessation of birth and
>   death.
> They who seek the *Ātman* by austerity, chastity, faith
>   and knowledge ...
> they do not return (to live another time-conditioned
>   existence).

> He who has understanding
> Who is mindful and ever pure,
> Reaches the goal
> From which he is born no more. (14)

In practical terms, it was taught that this knowledge might be attained by the techniques of *yoga*. These techniques enable their practitioner, the *yogi* or 'athlete of the spirit', to achieve detachment from the world and to attain the blessedness of union with Brahman. According to the authoritative description of Patanjali (c. 300 BC), yoga includes attentiveness towards God, called *Īśvara* or 'Ruler', the being who is totally free, unaffected by troubles, words and effects: in attending to him the devotee learns to accept all experience without resentment. Moreover by meditating on him, the being who is fundamentally free, the devotee discovers his own freedom and attains self-possession. (15) Although this religious element is present in some Hindu understanding of yoga, its motivation is primarily the attainment of self-mastery and inner freedom. The techniques and functions of yoga cover every facet of behaviour and form a coherent philosophy of the universe and man's place within it.

A classic statement of the methods and benefits of the yoga path is given in the Hindu *Bhagavad-Gītā*. 'When thought, held well in check, is stilled in self alone, then a man is freed from longing though all desires assail him, then do men call him "integrated". As a lamp might stand unflickering in a windless place so are those yogis who control their thought and practise integration of the self. When thought is checked by spiritual exercise and comes to rest, and when of one's self one sees the self in self (ātman) and finds content therein, that is the utmost joy which transcends all things of sense and which the soul alone can grasp ... Thus transcending all flaws, the athlete of the spirit, constant in integrating self, attains with ease unbounded joy, Brahman's saving touch.' (16)

Yoga does not imply a severe and unnatural asceticism, and the following description from the *Gītā* expresses the moderation and simplicity of the yoga way. 'Let the athlete of the spirit ever integrate himself, standing in a place apart, alone, his thoughts and self restrained, devoid of [earthly] hope, possessing nothing. Let him set up for himself a steady seat in a clean place, neither too high nor yet too low, covered with cloth or hide or grass. There let him sit and make his mind a single point, let him restrain the operations of his thought and senses and practise integration [yoga] to purify the self. Remaining still, let him keep body, head, and neck in a straight line, unmoving; let him fix his eye on the tip of his nose [or, 'between the eyebrows'], not looking round about him. There let him sit, his self all stilled, his fear all gone, firm in his vow of chastity, his mind controlled, his thoughts on me, integrated, [yet] intent on me. Thus let the yogi be constant in integrating himself, his mind restrained; then will he approach that peace which has *Nirvāna* as its end and which subsists in me.' (17)

The teachings of philosophical Hinduism (and the practice of yoga associated with them) seek man's response to the transcendent within the individual self and its growing relationship with the transcendent reality which lies behind all existence. The transcendent is identified with that which remains unchanged beneath the transient phenomena of the material world, and is eternally free and self-determined. The search for an enduring relationship with this unchanging ground of all being is expressed in the ancient Hindu prayer:

> From the unreal lead me to the real!
> From darkness lead me to the light!
> From death lead me to immortality! (18)

The teaching of the Upanishads about the relationship between ātman, the individual soul, and Brahman, the ground of all being, corresponds at some point with the insights of modern psychology that distinguish the conscious self from the higher self, the ego from the super-ego. For the true self comprises not only the unconscious elements of the individual personality but also those more mysterious elements by which the individual person is related to his community and to mankind, and is open to inspiration by forces outside himself. And in this awareness of the Self, as Jung and others have recognized, is the opportunity open to every human person of entering into a dynamic relationship with the eternal and the infinite. 'Like the sun whose rays radiate in every direction making life possible on earth, the rays of God's action and influence sustain everything in being from the largest of the giant stars to the tiniest neutron, from the trees of the forest to the fish in the ocean, from the lowly earth worm to man, made in God's image. The pressure of God's influence on each item of creation is towards its being itself and fulfilling its potential to the utmost of its capacity ... God acts on each and all of us through the world in which we live, through the people we meet, through our work and leisure, through our thinking and planning, through our dreams and through the unaccountable thoughts and impulses that push their way into consciousness.' (19) We stand each of us on one small shore of the great ocean and standing there find a kinship with it – in that kinship lies our peace and security even though it is but a single drop in those mighty waters.

Somewhat akin to Hindu teaching about the ātman-Brahman relationship is the teaching of Taoism about the way within nature which calls forth a corresponding response of humility and quietness in those who know that way. (20) Taoism is associated with particular Chinese scriptures, of which the most important is a book of poems, the *Tao Te Ching*, 'The Classic of the Way and the Power'. In the earliest general history of China, the *Shih Chi* (*Records of the Historian*), written in the first century BC, it is associated with Lao Tzu, a legendary figure who was supposed to have been a contemporary of Confucius.

There is further confusion with Lao Tau, who was treasurer of the Ch'u state about 374 BC, and who was associated with particular sayings in the book. In fact it is probably an anthology of wise sayings which originated round about 300 BC; like all anthologies it is not the work of a single author, and its chapters are somewhat disjointed. (21)

Tao, 'the Way', is the unchanging pattern of existence immanent in the universe from which all things come.

> Because the eye gazes but can catch no glimpse of it,
> It is called elusive.
> Because the ear listens but cannot hear it,
> It is called the rarefied.
> Because the hand feels for it but cannot find it,
> It is called the infinitesimal.
> These three, because they cannot be further scrutinized,
> Blend into one.
> Its rising brings no light;
> Its sinking, no darkness.
> Endless the series of things without name,
> On the way back to where there is nothing.
> They are called shapeless shapes;
> Forces without form;
> They are called vague semblances.
> Go towards them and you can see no front;
> Go after them, and you see no rear.
> Yet by seizing on the Way that was
> You can ride the things that are now.
> For to know what once there was, in the Beginning,
> This is called the essence of the Way. (22)

The poet thus expresses his wonder at the great mystery

beyond man's comprehension which lies behind all created things. '*Tao* is the ultimate reality in which all attributes are united, "it is heavy as a stone, light as a feather": it is the unity underlying plurality. "It is that by losing of which men die; by getting of which men live. Whatever is done without it, fails; whatever is done by means of it, succeeds. It has neither root nor stalk, leaf nor flower. Yet upon it depends the generation and the growth of the ten thousand things, each after its kind."' But 'no term can be applied to the Tao because all terms are specific, and the specific, if applied to the Tao, will impose a limitation on the range of its functions. And the Tao that is limited in its function can no longer serve as the Tao that sustains the manifold universe.' (23)

Since all other things issue from this great mystery of primal existence, they must be used with modesty. All attributes are, by comparison with Tao itself, only of relative value and nothing is absolutely great, or strong or magnificent. The way of wisdom is to accept nature as it is, and to conduct oneself humbly and quietly as a child towards it. To accept the fundamental equilibrium in nature, which is expressed in Tao, is to use the power (*te*) which is associated with it. Thus in the exercise of arts and skills, craftsmen, artists and athletes succeed, not by brute force, but by going with the way of the universe, quiet, serene, all-pervasive. This principle is true for the whole universe, both in its creation and its maintenance.

Of old, these came to be in possession of the One:
Heaven in virtue of the One is limpid;
Earth in virtue of the One is settled;
Gods in virtue of the One have their potencies;

45

The valley in virtue of the One is full;
The myriad creatures in virtue of the One are alive;
Lords and princes in virtue of the One become leaders
    in the empire.
It is the One that makes these what they are.

In these verses 'the One' is used as a synonym for Tao,
the Way. (24)

Man's happiness consists in discovering for himself the
Tao, and reflecting in his own life the same 'inaction', the
same 'non-competition in emptiness', the same serenity,
which are the characteristics of Tao itself. When a person
is free from desire, has emptiness of spirit and acts simply
by following the way of nature, he can know and attain
contentment. The primal undifferentiated unity which
underlies the apparent complexity of the universe is 'the
Uncarved Block' which men may hold and thereby find
peace and serenity.

If ... men find life too plain and unadorned,
Then let them have accessories.
Give them Simplicity [literally 'raw silk'] to look at,
the Uncarved Block to hold,
Give them selflessness and pureness of desires. (25)

This is not a comprehensive account of Taoism, which
over the centuries has been mixed with the traditional
religions of China and with some aspects of *Mahāyāna*
Buddhism (26); but this description illustrates that aspect
of man's response to the transcendent which is seen also
in philosophical Hinduism. Man perceives a deep and
abiding reality behind the manifold phenomena of experience – a relationship, a tenuous congruence linking all that

happens – and he believes it to be the source of all that exists and the ground on which everything else depends: he seeks within himself for a close relationship with this infinite and eternal reality.

3. *A Stream of Sweet Water*

In contrast with philosophical Hinduism and classical Taoism which speak of the transcendent in largely impersonal terms are Judaism, Christianity and Islam. They are closely related to each other, in their Semitic origins, their attachment to Jerusalem, and in the relationships between their adherents over many centuries. We shall later in this book notice some of the differences between them, but for the moment I emphasize the common affirmation which they make of the personal nature of God, his sovereignty over creation and the obligations and obedience which his creatures owe to him. Nowhere is this affirmation more clearly made than in the daily prayer-act, the *ṣalāt*, which Islam has developed as the universal duty for all Muslims. One of the Five Pillars of the Faith, the ṣalāt is the most constant expression in daily life of the 'service to God' which is the key to Muslim theology and behaviour. Man's highest status is that he is *'abdu llāh*, 'the servant of God', a title of honour given by the Qur'ān to Christ and to Muhammad as well as to others.

The prayer-act should be performed five times each day, and they corresponding roughly with dawn, mid-day, the afternoon, sunset and nightfall. At each of these times the call to prayer is proclaimed from the minarets of the mosques. Even the person who prays by himself at home or in the field is expected to begin his prayer with a recitation of the call to prayer.

It is as follows:

God is most great:
I testify that there is no god except God:
I testify that Muhammad is the apostle of God:
Come to prayer:
Come to prosperity:
God is most great:
There is no god except God.

The first phrase is repeated four times, all the others, except the last, twice; at the dawn prayer, the phrase 'prayer is better than sleep' is repeated after 'come to prosperity'. When the call is made publicly, those who hear it are expected to respond to it by reciting the phrases after the *mu'adhdhin*. When praying, Muslims face in the direction of the *Ka'ba*, the House of God, in Mecca and this gives them the sense of belonging to one community, though one which is scattered all over the world. Their sense of community is strengthened still more by the practice of marshalling the worshippers in ranks without gaps or spaces; there is no room for personal preference as in so many Christian churches. Women at the mosque services, however, stand in the back rows.

The Muslim is taught to prepare himself carefully for the act of prayer; he must first wash at least his face, hands and feet, and then select a clean piece of ground on which to pray or use a prayer-mat. It is also recommended that if a person intends to pray in a mosque he should go there and wait quietly some time before the time of prayer, and that he should make a deliberate mental affirmation of his intention to perform the prayer-act. During the performance of the ṣalāt the Muslim follows a prescribed series of different postures, including prostration, each of which expresses in a different way attention, humility and devotion to God. (27)

The prayers used are of several kinds including recitation of passages from the Qur'ān, the ejaculation of short praise sentences – 'God is most great' and 'I proclaim the praise of my Lord, the Almighty', for example, and prayers for forgiveness and for blessing. The latter might be: 'O God, separate me from my sins as you have separated the east from the west. O God, cleanse me from my sins as the white robe is cleansed from stain. O God, cleanse me from my sins with water, and snow and hail.' The most commonly used passage from the Qur'ān is the opening chapter, *al-Fātiḥa*.

Praise be to God,
Lord of the Universe,
The Merciful, the Compassionate,
Sovereign of the Day of Judgement.
You are the One we worship:
You are the One we ask for help.
Guide us along the straight highway,
the highway of those who receive your grace,
not that of those who incur anger or who go astray.

The prayer-act as practised in Islam involves the whole personality in its performance, the mind in the acts of recollection and recitation, the body in the adoption of the different postures required, and the inner self in the attitudes of humility and dependence induced by the prayers. It is, moreover, a disciplined act in which the whole congregation takes an active part from beginning to end; standing behind the *'imām*, they follow his actions and utter the prayers and praises with him. At the same time, the prayer-act may be performed in any place which is ritually clean; thus wherever he is, in his shop or his garden, at home or visiting others, by the road side or on the building site, the Muslim is able to participate in the great offering of prayer which is constantly being made throughout the Islamic world. It is an act of devotion for all, and does not depend on the presence of anyone specially trained in religion. (28)

The following passage, from a modern handbook, describes the effects of the prayer-rite as follows. 'The true practice of the prayer-rite, which is built upon humility and submissiveness, illuminates the heart and polishes the soul; it teaches the worshipper the proper practice of worship, and the duties which he owes to God his Lord, because it implants in his heart something of the majesty of God and his greatness: it ennobles a man and endows him with the noblest virtues like integrity, trustworthiness, contentment, gentleness, modesty, justice, goodness: it elevates the one who prays, directs him towards God alone and causes him to wait much upon him and to fear him; thus his ambition becomes lofty, his soul thrives, and he is elevated far above lying, perfidy, evil, treachery, anger and pride, and raised above adultery, injustice, meanness, corruption and rebellion.' (29)

This daily five-fold practice of prayer has, down through the centuries, nurtured and fostered the God-awareness of the Muslim communities, and purified men's lives. In the words of a tradition attributed to Muhammad, 'the ṣalāt is like a stream of sweet water which flows past the door of each one of you; into it a man plunges five times a day: do you think that anything remains of his uncleanness after that?' But this stream of sweet water is one which

flows across the world and into which people of many
different religious communities plunge for cleansing.
Prayer is, for people of all religions, an unfailing source of
strength and courage, the way to life and the means of
communion with the eternal Spirit whose presence is disclosed to them. The Qur'ān itself may allude to Christian
as well as Muslim places of worship in the following verses
which have been a source of inspiration to many, especially
the Ṣūfī mystics.

> God is the Light of the heavens and the earth: ...
> [He is] Light upon Light, and God guides to his
> Light whoever he wills ...
> He permits temples to be raised, in which his name is
> mentioned,
> and praises to be offered to him at morning and at
> evening ...
> Have you not seen that whoever is in heaven and
> earth praises God, even the birds spreading their
> wings?
> Each one: he knows its prayer and its praises. God knows
> what they do. (30)

4. A Thousand Names – One God

Humans have always sought to name their gods, for to
know the name of another is to have some influence upon
him. To know a person's name gives one the means by
which to address him, to summon him for help, to make
claims upon him. Conversely, to reveal one's identity to
another is to build a living relationship with the other,
and to give of one's friendship to him. Thus the many
personal names used in prayer reflect the manifold ex-

periences of humanity in their diverse encounters with the
eternal and the transcendent.

Most common of all are names which describe the
different *activities* of God in relation to the universe, as
in this ancient Hebrew psalm.

Praise the Lord,
the one who pardons all my guilt,
the one who heals all my disease,
the one who rescues me from the pit [of death],
the one who makes me glad with constant love and tender
   affection,
the one who fills my years with goodness, so that my youth
   is renewed like an eagle's. (31)

This way of naming God is similar to the 'collect' which
has been in constant use in the Christian Church, first in
Latin and then in other languages. The collect is usually
addressed to God and then some statement about him is
added on the grounds of which a specific petition is made
to him. Typical examples are these: 'Almighty God, who
showest to them that be in error the light of thy truth ...';
'Almighty God, who alone canst order the unruly wills
and affections of sinful men ...'; 'O Lord, from whom
all good things do come ...'. (32)

In Islam, recitation of 'the names of God' has been a
practice of popular religion through the centuries and the
phrases used in this way are very varied. The most commonly used are ninety-nine in number and are known as 'the
most beautiful names', in Arabic *al-'asmā'u l-ḥusnā*. (33)
Examples are: the Finder, the Beginner, the Creator,
the Fashioner, the Protector, the Sustainer, the Enricher,
the Director to the Right Way, the Answerer (of prayer).

There are also *epithets* which describe God as his worshippers conceive him to be. Such epithets fall into three main classes. First, some describe the majesty and greatness of God as he is pictured in human imagination: Muslim examples are the Great, the Powerful, the Strong, the Possessor of Majesty, the Eternal, the Knower, the Hearer, the See-er, and these are counterparts to the Christian usage, Almighty and Everlasting God.

Other epithets describe the moral qualities which are associated with the being to whom worship is offered. A Hebrew psalm illustrates this association:

Lord, your constant love reaches the heavens;
your faithfulness extends to the skies.
Your righteousness is towering like the mountains;
your justice is like the depths of the sea. (34)

Similar epithets appear in the Islamic names; the Wise, the Merciful, the Compassionate, the Forgiver, the Generous, the Patient, the Benign, the Loving. Yet other epithets describe the relationship between God and the creation. The most common of these are King, Lord, and Father, and in one form or another they recur throughout the religions. They are developed with rich diversity in the Hindu *Bhagavad-Gītā*.

Gabriel M. Setiloane, an African, wrote a long poem wrestling with the relationship between his ancestral faith and Christianity. In the course of it he wrote:

My fathers and theirs, many generations before, knew Him.
They bowed the knee to Him,

By many names they knew Him,
And yet 'tis He the One and only God.
They called Him:
UVELINGQAKI:
  The First One
  Who came ere ever anything appeared:
UNKULUNKULU:
  The BIG BIG ONE,
  So big indeed that no space would ever contain Him.
MODIMO:
  Because His abode is far up in the sky.
They also knew Him as MODIRI:
  For He has made all;
and LESA:
  The spirit without which the breath of man cannot be.

(35)

These many varied names demonstrate the manifold nature of the experience of God, and the fact that God is known primarily as he is experienced in human life. They demonstrate also how little men claim to know of God as he is in himself. The mystery of God is a constant cause for wonder and this is reflected in the names which suggest the difficulty of knowing God or predicting his actions. Thus, for example, the Toussian tribe of West Africa name the Supreme Being *Liyele*, 'He who cannot be understood', 'the Variable', 'the Wanderer'. (36)

But my fathers, from the mouth of their fathers, say
That this God of old shone
With a brightness so bright
It blinded them ... (35)

54

In most religions, one particular name is used for 'God', and this name in turn becomes so all-inclusive as to need further definition by subsidiary names and epithets. The Maori of New Zealand, for example, called their 'High God' *Io*, which means 'the innermost part', and thought of Io as the supreme power, present in the world, and alive before all other living things; to this name they added others.

Io Matua: the parent father.
Io Matua-kore: having no parents.
Io Mata-ngaro: face that cannot be seen.
Io Wanango: source of all knowledge.
Io Te Waiora: the spring-water of life. (37)

By contrast, the Dinka of the Sudan use *Nhialic*, which means 'the one who is above, in the sky'. (38) The Hebrew name for God used in the Old Testament, *Yahweh*, means 'he who will always be there', and it also could be joined with other words. (39)

The Muslim name for God, *Allāh*, asserts in its simplicity the uniqueness of the divine being, the general opinion of Arabic scholarship being that it is a contraction of *al-'ilāh*, meaning 'the [only] god'. Thus the first half of the Muslim declaration of faith declares *lā 'ilāha 'illa llāh*, 'there is no god except the [only] god', or 'there is no god except Allāh'. Allāh is, in developed Muslim theology, the unique transcendent being who has no peer or associate, and who is the sovereign disposer and lord of all created beings and things. But this simplicity does not suffice either to express the manifold ways in which people become aware of God's presence or their expectations of him. He becomes real to people in a thousand different ways and they respond by using a thousand different names.

5. The Way of Renunciation

In the previous two sections we have considered responses to the transcendent which describe the relationship between God and his creatures in personal terms. Philosophical Hinduism and classical Taoism explain the relationship in largely impersonal terms, though sometimes Brahman was given personal titles, such as Lord and King, and in some Taoist writings the Tao is addressed with the commitment of trust and love. We turn now to Buddhism, which is different from most other religions in that it says little about any relationship of dependence or worship. Its whole emphasis is upon the *Dharma*, the Truth taught by the Buddha, in which renunciation and self-discipline lead in the end to enlightenment and to Nirvāna. It is a path which the believer is called to tread alone, though drawing strength from the teaching of the Buddha: 'One is one's own refuge,' said the Buddha; 'do not look to another for refuge.' (40)

The following account, which includes legendary as well as historical material, narrates in a few paragraphs the received tradition of the Buddha's life upon which Buddhists build their religious teaching and their behaviour.

Gautama Siddhārtha was born of a princely family in the sixth century BC, in eastern India. He was brought up as a Hindu in circumstances of wealth and luxury and married to his wife Yasodharā at sixteen. For thirteen years after his marriage he led a life of luxury and happiness. He was an educated man, and skilled in many pursuits. Had he wished, he could have continued to live in these circumstances.

Gautama Siddhārtha was troubled, however, by contact with old age, sickness, death and poverty. The traditional accounts of his life dramatize his growing awareness of these facets of human experience, in particular incidents which forced themselves on the notice of the young prince as he drove by in his chariot. He became aware of suffering within human experience, and, in accordance with the Hindu teaching in which he had been brought up, he longed to win freedom from the unending cycle of existence (*saṁsāra*), marked as it is by change and suffering. 'There is a getting born and a growing old, a dying and a being reborn. But, alas, no escape is known from this suffering, not even from old age and death.' At the age of twenty-nine, he left home in search of this freedom and began to live the life of a 'holy man'.

During the next six years Gautama Siddhārtha sought deliverance. He practised yoga with two teachers in Bihar but, disappointed at the results, he left them to live a more ascetic life with five beggars. At times his life was endangered by the extremes of ascetic practice which he followed. Finding no salvation in this, he gave up fasting, whereupon his five friends left him.

At last on a full-moon night in May, he sat under a tree to meditate. His long efforts for salvation, including according to Buddhist teaching those in very many previous existences, were rewarded; despite a final struggle with *Māra*, the Evil One, the tempter, he achieved complete and final enlightenment. He became at that moment 'the Enlightened One', the Buddha. The year, according to European scholars, was about 531 BC, although Indian traditions vary by as much as three hundred years earlier or later. (41)

'He discovered the ultimate reality of things and the final goal of existence. He had grasped the principle of causation, and finally convinced himself of the lack of self in all that is.' (42)

For the next forty-five years the Buddha taught what he had learned of human existence and the means of enlightenment, or salvation. He travelled incessantly throughout north India, in the regions of the middle Ganges, teaching and making many converts. Then, at the age of eighty, he relinquished his mortal existence and entered into the state of Nirvāna, 'like the flame which dies for lack of fuel', where he lives in unending bliss and glory. Buddhist art depicts mostly this now 'glorified body' of the Buddha with its thirty-two 'marks of a superman', and brilliant light emanating from it on all sides. This reflects Buddhist belief that the Buddha-nature was within Gautama from his youth, inspiring him to understand and teach the truth, and that this same Buddha-nature manifests itself from time to time in the world through others (both before and after Gautama), who also achieve enlightenment and preach the same doctrine. (43)

The Dharma, the Truth as taught by the Buddha, is summed up in the four principles known as the Four Noble Truths. These lie at the centre of all the varied schools of Buddhist thought and are traditionally the substance of the sermon which the Buddha preached in the presence of the five beggars whom he met again after his enlightenment.

The Four Noble Truths are these:

The Truth about Suffering: The whole experience of life, in body and in mind, is marked by sorrow. The phenomena of existence are transitory, constantly changing, and because of their impermanence they cause sorrow and pain; even a transient happiness which is doomed to disappear is in the end painful to the one who expects lasting happiness. All things carry within them the element of suffering, associated with pain, decay and death. Sorrow is the greater because it is experienced in every one of successive existences. 'While in this long journey you wander at random from migration to migration and sigh and weep because your portion is what you hate while you are deprived of what you love, you have shed more tears than there is water in the four heavens.' (44)

The Truth about the Origin of Suffering: The cause of suffering is the desires which produce the actions that occasion suffering. The phenomena of existence associated with suffering take place by acts of the will prompted by desire: the desire may be the craving for pleasure, or the desire, based on illusion, either for continued existence or for annihilation in death. The law of *karma*, by which all actions have their consequences, taken over from Hinduism, perpetuates this suffering through many consecutive existences.

The Truth about the Stopping of Suffering: There is a form of existence which is unconditioned and in no way linked with desire or impermanence. This is the blissful state of Nirvāna, in which there is no suffering because there is no desire for the impermanent phenomena which occasion suffering. The saint who has destroyed desire and withdrawn wholly from the craving for existence and for pleasure, knows Nirvāna in this world and at the end of his mortal existence enters into endless peace.

The Truth about the Way to Nirvāna. There is a Way by which a man can set himself free from the passions and desires which are the cause of suffering, and thus attain Nirvāna. It is the Noble Eightfold Path taught by the Buddha, the Middle Way between the two extremes of self-indulgence and self-torture. (45)

This account of the doctrine of Buddhism is the one most familiar to Western scholars and enquirers and it concentrates on the basic teaching of the Buddha and his immediate followers. It remains at the heart of the many different developments within Buddhism, although, as Buddhism has spread across Asia in the past 2500 years, many different Buddhist schools have come into being. (46)

Can Buddhism be counted as a religion, since it does not teach the existence of a supreme personal being upon whom the world is dependent for life and salvation, or who created the universe? In this sense, Buddhism is not a religion, even though in popular Buddhism people make prayers and offerings in the hope of winning help from the objects of their worship. But Buddhism gives the promise of Nirvāna, the permanent and imperishable, 'the harbour of refuge', 'the cool cave', 'the island amidst the floods', 'the end of suffering', 'the supreme joy', as the ultimate Good and the Supreme Reality. The Dharma (Truth) which the Buddha taught is also a transcendent reality whose claims on those who practise it are absolute. Moreover the Buddha in his glorified state is the personal embodiment of Nirvāna, and the object of veneration, endless love and trust. (47) In this sense, therefore, Buddhism is certainly a religion, for it seeks to regulate the whole of life, and it teaches a Way by which the Buddhist may himself achieve final enlightenment. It deals with the ultimate things of life and it points its followers towards the absolute and the transcendent.

NOTES

1. E. E. Evans-Pritchard, *Nuer Religion*, Oxford, 1956: also C. G. and B. Z. Seligman, *Pagan Tribes of the Nilotic Sudan*, London, 1932, 206 ff.

2. This summary is taken from Evans-Pritchard's book, especially chapter 1 (his 1951 Presidential Address to the Royal Anthropological Institute), and chapter XIII.

3. See e.g. G. Parrinder, *Religion in Africa*, Penguin, 1969, 45 and 24.

4. Ruth Benedict, *Patterns of Culture*, London, Routledge, 1935, 15.

5. John V. Taylor, *The Primal Vision*, SCM Press, 1963, 75–6.

6. H. Gravrand, *Meeting the African Religions*, Rome, 1968, 43–4.

7. For a brief description of the key words used see R. C. Zaehner, *Hinduism*, Oxford, 1966, 4–6.

8. Zaehner, op. cit., 61–3.

9. *Chāndogya Upanishad*, V, X, 7–8 in *Hindu Scriptures*, edited by R. C. Zaehner, Everyman's Library, edit. of 1966, 101

10. Zaehner, op. cit., 60.
11. Op. cit., 49–50, and 80.
12. See A. C. Bouquet, *Hinduism*, Hutchinson, 2nd Edit., 1962, 43–50: R. E. Hume, *The Thirteen Principal Upanishads*, Oxford, 2nd Edit., 1931, 1–72: *Hindu Scriptures*, edited by R. C. Zaehner, VIII-XV.
13. Zaehner, op. cit., 67–81.
14. Hume, op. cit., 57 and 61.
15. See especially Ernest Wood, *Yoga*, Penguin Books, 1959, a comprehensive introduction to the subject with an extensive bibliography, and especially 18 and 43–5.
16. *Bhagavad-Gītā* 6. 18–28. This translation is from that by R. C. Zaehner, Oxford, 1969: other translations are by W. D. P. Hill, Oxford, 1953; J. Mascaro, Penguin, 1962; G. Parrinder, Sheldon Press, 1974.
17. 6. 10–17.
18. *Bṛihad-aranyaka Upanishad*, 1, iii, 28 in *Hindu Scriptures* (R. C. Zaehner), 34.
19. See C. Bryant, *The River Within*, London, 1978, 10–13, 79.
20. For both Taoism and Confucianism I have relied mainly on the following:
    (i) Chapter 9, contributed by Tongshik Ryu, in *A Guide to Religions*, edited David Brown, SPCK, 1975.
    (ii) Part II, chapter 6, by V. Che-chen-tao and Part III, chapter 2, by J. Shih, S. J., in *Religions*, Rome, Ancora, 1970.
    (iii) Arthur Waley, *The Way and its Power*, London, Allen and Unwin, 1934.
    (iv) D. C. Lau, *Lao Tzu, Tao Te Ching*, London, Penguin, 1963.

(*v*) Articles in E. Royston Pike, *Encyclopaedia of Religions*, London, Allen and Unwin, 1951.

21. See particularly Waley, op. cit., 101–8 and 121–32, and Lau, op. cit., 1–14, 147–74.

22. *Tao Te Ching*, chapter 14. This and other translations from the same book are taken from Waley (W) as here, or Lau (L).

23. Waley, 50–51: Lau, 19.

24. Ch. 39 (L).

25. Ch. 19 (W).

26. See the article by J. Shih in *Religions*, 259–94.

27. A good description with diagrams is in E. Lane, *The Manners and Customs of the Modern Egyptians*, Everyman's Library, 1908 and reprinted, 77–81.

28. See Kenneth Cragg, *The Dome and the Rock*, SPCK, 1964, 18.

29. This passage and other details are taken from an Arabic text book published in 'Ammān: M. Maḥmūd al-Ṣawāf, *Ta'līm al-Ṣalāt*, 8th Edit., page 10.

30. Q. 24. 35–6, 41.

31. Psalm 103. 3–5. The translation, based on the NEB, is my own.

32. *Book of Common Prayer*, the 3rd, 4th and 5th Sundays after Easter.

33. A full list is given in the article 'Allāh' in *The Encyclopaedia of Islam*.

34. Psalm 36. 5–6.

35. *Uniting in Hope*, WCC, Geneva, 1975, 59.

36. Gravrand, op. cit., 178.

37. Ruawai Rakena, 'The Maori', chapter 5, in *A Guide to Religions*.

38. Godfrey Lienhardt, *Divinity and Experience*, Oxford, 1961, 29–30.

39. Exodus 3. 13–15: 17. 15: Jeremiah 33. 16: 1 Samuel 17. 45.

40. From David Young, in *Face to Face*, London, Highway Press, 1971, 55.

41. For a simple account of his life see Lynn de Silva in *Guide to Religions*, 123–6, and Etienne Lamotte, *Towards the Meeting with Buddhism*, Ancora, Rome, 1970, vol. 1, 13–17. A traditional account of his life is in *Buddhist Scriptures*, edited by Edward Conze, Penguin Books, 1959, 36–66.

42. *Buddhist Scriptures*, 49, 51.

43. For the 'glorified body' of the Buddha and its significance, see E. Conze, *Buddhism*, Oxford (Bruno Cassirer), 3rd Edit., 1957, 36–8: *Buddhist Scriptures*, 19–20.

44. Quoted by Lamotte, op. cit., 21.

45. For the Eightfold Path see further chapter 4, pages 114 ff. For a summary of the sermon see Lamotte, op. cit., I, 17–30: *Buddhist Scriptures*, 186–7.

46. Especially *Towards the Meeting with Buddhism*, volume II.

47. See Conze, op. cit, 39 ff: P. Humbertclaude, in *Towards etc.*, II, 99; *A Guide to Religions*, 145 ff.

CHAPTER 3

Word

Common to all religions is awareness of a reality, complex and mysterious, that transcends the whole range of human experience and, itself independent and unchanging, sustains the universe in being. It is possible to enter into a life-sustaining relationship with this transcendent reality, either of the personal kind affirmed by Christianity, Islam, and some of the traditional religions, or in the more impersonal ways taught in Hinduism and Taoism. Even in Buddhism the disciple is confronted by the Truth which makes demands upon him. In this awareness of the transcendent worship is primarily not search but response: it is the Other who takes the initiative and calls for an answer. In this chapter we consider the different ways in which God is believed to reveal his will and his nature to men.

1. *The Heavens Declare*

Man comes to know the divine presence through the natural universe in which he lives. From earliest times, people have been aware of the strange powers which operate in sky and weather, in birth and death, and have felt their dependence upon the changes of the seasons, the alternation of night and day ruled by moon and sun, the coming of rain and wind, the pull of the tides and the filling of the rivers. It was in this context that belief developed in the spirits and divinities which men worship and upon which they feel dependent; and men have had to work out the expression of that belief, and their relationship with its object. At early periods in the development of human thought, this was done by means of myths, which give a quasi-rational explanation of the complexity of the natural universe. Natural forces, for example, often appeared to be in conflict with each other and this needed to be 'explained' in one way or another. In making these explanations, people drew on their experience of the social institutions which they were developing at the same time as their religious ones. Thus in different ways, through their efforts both to understand their natural environment and to cope with it, and also to build healthy and strong communities, men have been led to extend and to deepen their religious ideas.

In this section I give three examples of different ways in which humans have perceived in the natural universe indications of the transcendent.

I

The earliest section of the Hindu scriptures, the *Rig-Veda*, consists of more than a thousand hymns addressed to the gods. They originated at a very early period, around 1500–1000 BC, when the Nordic Aryans invaded India from the north-west and conquered its indigenous peoples. There are links between the religion of the Rig-Veda and those of other Indo-European peoples, both in Iran and further to the west in Greece and Rome, and it is possible that later developments in Hinduism represent a recovery of influence by the indigenous peoples. The hymns of the Rig-Veda were composed and revised over a long period of time and they do not present a coherent theology but one which is constantly changing and developing.

Speaking generally, the deities named in the Rig-Veda are identified with forces and powers in the natural universe. *Agni* is the god of fire, who brings blessings to men, and links earth with heaven through the fire of sacrifice, *Soma* is associated with the plant *soma* whose intoxicating juice was drunk in sacrifice and gave long life to gods and men, *Indra* is associated with the rain, and *Ushas* with the dawn. 'The divine powers believed in and worshipped by these early Nordic colonists are Powers of Nature in the first instance, and there is to begin with no idea of a single supreme Godhead. Indeed the primary notion seems to be that of a plurality of Powers, not even personal ones, but connected with the various objects, occurrences or episodes of daily life. The name of the thing or the circumstance is the name of the god. Thus Agni is Fire, and gradually He of the Fire ... It is only as the physical basis of this divinity tends to be forgotten that the god comes to be fully personified.' (1) The Brāhmin's daily prayer is: 'We meditate on the lovely light of the god, *Savitṛi* [a sun-god]: May it stimulate our thoughts.' (2)

The following hymn to Agni, the god of fire, illustrates the praise and prayer element of the Vedic hymns. Alluding to the many uses of fire, in homemaking, in metal-work and in sacrifice, the hymn presents a dynamic mythological picture of the natural universe in which gods and men share together.

I praise Agni, the chosen priest, god, minister of sacrifice, most lavish of wealth.
Worthy is Agni to be praised by living as by ancient

seers; he shall bring hitherward the gods.

Through Agni man obtaineth wealth, yea plenty, waxing
day by day;

Most rich in heroes, glorious.

Agni, the perfect sacrifice which thou encompassest
about verily goeth to the gods.

May Agni, sapient-minded priest, truthful, most glori-
ously great,

The god, come hither with the gods ...

To thee, dispeller of the night, O Agni, day by day with
prayer bringing thee reverence, we come.

Ruler of sacrifices, guard of law eternal, radiant one,
increasing in thine own abode.

Be to us easy of approach, even as a father to his son;
Agni, be with us for our weal. (3)

In other Indo-European religions one deity often emerged
to become the undisputed 'king of gods and men', as *Zeus*
did in Greece, *Jupiter* in Rome and *Ahura-mazda* in Iran.
In the *Vedas* this process is absent and instead 'the deities'
tend to coalesce the one into the other, and in so doing
they lose their identity and indeed their relevance. The
supreme principle is felt to be one, and it does not matter
very much what you call it: "They call it Indra, Mitra,
Varuna, Fire; or again it is the celestial bird Garutmat.
What is but one the wise call [by] manifold [names]".' (*Rig-
Veda*, I. CLXIV. 46) (4) Nevertheless virtually supreme
powers and dignity were associated at different times with
one or other of the gods, and in particular with *Varuṇa*
until he was displaced by *Indra,* the warrior god. This
usurpation may reflect social changes within India over
a long period of time. (5)

Through the centuries since the final compilation of the

Rig-Veda there have been many changes within Hinduism. Later the teachings of the Upanishads affirmed the reality of the one eternal being, Brahman, and other developments were to follow. But the Rig-Veda remains the most sacred of all Hindu scriptures and is a fundamental element in Hindu theology and worship.

II

Although the Rig-Veda was compiled nearly three thousand years ago, the response which its hymns express to the forces in nature and in society with which man's life is enmeshed is echoed in the traditional religions of our own age. They also identify the dominant phenomena in the natural universe as forces on which men's lives depend and with which they seek to build good relations. The Dinka, to take one example, are a tribal group of nearly a million people living in the swamps and flat country near to the White Nile and its western tributaries. Their main wealth and interest lie in their cattle which the men herd in temporary cattle camps during most of the year, according to the flow of water in the rivers and streams. During the rainy season they grow small crops of grain and vegetables near their more permanent homesteads.

The powers which the Dinka worship are generally referred to as *Nhialic*, 'That which is above in the sky', though individually they are called *jok*, 'spirits' or 'powers'. Nhialic is used both for 'the sky' and also as a personal name for the greatest of the powers who is both 'creator and father'. But associated with Nhialic are a number of other divinities. They represent some of the natural elements which are of the greatest significance to the Dinka. Thus *Deng*, or *Dengdit*, is associated with rain (*deng*), thunder and lightning, and there are a few sanctuaries associated with Deng, at which sacrifice is offered. *Garang* is associated with the colours, red and brown, which mark the cattle; it is also the name of the first man. *Abuk* is a kindly deity and associated especially with women. *Macardit*, 'the great, black one', is a harmful power, and associated with the evil influences which hurt men. It is a personification of all the contrary and haphazard circumstances of ill-chance which threaten human well-being.

Together with these major deities, every clan has its own divinity or divinities, which are represented by particular emblems. These emblems include many kinds of animals, birds, insects and trees, and also larger objects like the forest, the rain, the River Nile and the planet Venus. Sacrifices and prayers are offered to these divinities, often to a number of them at the same time, in the homesteads of the Dinka, by the priests, who are known as 'masters of the [sacred] fishing spears'.

Dinka religion appears at first sight haphazard and confusing, but it is an elaborate system of belief and conduct which has evolved over a long period of time. It expresses, in a mythological form, the way in which the Dinka apprehend the complexity and mystery of the environment which surrounds them, and it enables them to make the fundamental religious responses of worship and of prayer. There are no images as such, the focus of worship being the sacred spears and particular places in the homesteads marked out in different ways as places for sacrifice. (6)

Dinka names and mythology are peculiar to themselves and they developed within the extreme isolation in which the Dinka have lived for centuries, though there are close similarities with the Nuer, their immediate neighbours in the Upper Nile region of the Sudan. But the basic pattern is repeated elsewhere in comparable situations. In Ghana, for example, the traditional religion of the Ga people near Accra, names *Naa Nyonmo* as the great creator spirit, but associates with him a variety of others, the *dzemawodzi* ('the gods of the world'), to whom he has delegated his authority. Each Ga clan has its own divinity, but senior among them are *Nae*, the sea-god, and *Afiyee*, his wife; *Sakumo*, a river-god and the god who leads in war; *La Kpa*, a lagoon-god, and *Ashi Akle* a sea-goddess. *Nae* is the chief deity and worshipped at a sanctuary near the sea. There are also many lesser deities and spirit-powers. (7)

These two sections illustrate the response which people make to the transcendent as they perceive its presence and influence in the universe around them. The worship of the Vedic and other gods has continued in India through the centuries alongside the teachings of the Upanishads and the *Gītā*, and respect for the traditional religions is growing with our greater knowledge of them. In both cases we have noted the tendency to recognize one transcendent being behind particular deities and powers. Yet the worship represented both in the Vedas and in the traditional religions has severe limitations in so far as it is directed towards the creation rather than the creator. To worship created things and natural forces, however majestic or powerful, in the end stultifies growth in religious knowledge and moral conduct since the object worshipped is itself part of the finite universe. Where images are used, as in Hinduism and in some but not all of the traditional religions, another factor becomes important. Although for many worshippers the image or statue is recognized to be no more than a symbol, or ikon, of the deity or transcendent reality to which worship is offered, their mutual association is often so strong that for many the image itself becomes the object of worship and of trust. Moreover, because worship is offered to things which cannot, by their nature, respond to their worshippers, response is made by the guardians or priests who control access to the shrines. Unless some wider vision of truth commands their loyalty, they can easily manipulate religious practices to their own ends, and the result has often been superstition and oppression.

III

Before the advent of Christianity and Islam, the religions of many peoples in the Middle East were of this general kind. They worshipped a plurality of deities representative of forces and powers in nature, or personifications of their own national or civic identities. Some Jewish kings attempted to establish in Israel the worship of *Ba'al*, the storm-god of the Syrians, and of *Astarte*, goddess of fertility, his consort. In the Greek and Roman periods the old cults of Syria were adapted to the deities of Greece and Rome, and on several occasions attempts were again made to establish some of them in Jerusalem. The Arab tribes also worshipped a multiplicity of deities, and the characteristic mark of their religion during the Age of Ignorance, according to Muhammad, was the sin of *shirk*, associating other deities with the one and only God. (8)

Both the Rig-Veda and the traditional religions demonstrate the tendency to acknowledge one supreme deity behind the many who are worshipped. But it was the supreme achievement of the Jews during the Old Testament period, and subsequently of Muhammad in pagan Arabia, to affirm the reality of the one living God, the only creator of the whole universe, and his unconditioned sovereignty over all the powers and forces of the created universe. In making this affirmation, they declared uncompromising opposition to any form of idolatry, or any attempt to portray the being of God in the likeness of any creature.

The LORD, the holy God of Israel,
the one who shapes the future, says: ...
'I am the one who made the earth
and created mankind to live there.
By my power I stretched out the heavens;
I control the sun, the moon, and the stars ...
I am the LORD, and there is no other God ...
I am the LORD and I speak the truth;
I make known what is right.'
To whom can God be compared?
How can you describe what he is like?
He is not like an idol that workmen make,
that metalworkers cover with gold and set in a base of
silver ...
To whom can the holy God be compared?
Is there anyone else like him?

Invoke the name of your Lord and devote yourself entirely to him:
He is Lord of the East and the West:
There is no god except he – so take him for your protector. (9)

Affirmation of the sole existence of one living God, however, went side by side with the belief that men may meet with God through the processes of nature, or of history. Since the universe came into existence through the creative activity of God, it expresses his purposes, and, in so far as it may be known through his actions, his nature also.

The Old Testament scriptures provide ample evidence of this belief in many of the psalms and in some of the prophets. The glad shout of praise, 'How clearly the sky reveals God's glory! How plainly it shows what he has done!', is echoed by the declaration which Amos, the shepherd turned prophet, made about *Yahweh*, the God of Israel: 'It is he who forges the thunder and creates the wind, who showers abundant rain on the earth, who darkens the dawn with thick clouds and marches over the heights of the earth – his name is the Lord the God of Hosts.' In the opening chapter of the second half of the book of Isaiah the prophet declares the God of mountain, plain, wind and rain to be the God who cares for Israel, his people. (10)

The Wisdom writers of the Old Testament also emphasized the order apparent in nature, and its importance as one means by which God calls men to seek that same order in human society. 'Wisdom, which we have understood as the primeval world order, as the mystery behind the creation of the world ... is orientated towards man, offering him help; it is concerned about him, indeed addresses him directly ... Creation not only exists, it also discharges truth.' This Old Testament insight is a background to much of the teaching of Jesus. He often referred to the natural world and used it to illustrate God's generosity and his fatherly providence. (11)

A similar sympathetic openness towards the natural

world as one means by which God reveals himself to men is prominent in the Qur'ān. God's works in creation, and his sustaining presence within the whole natural order, provide 'signs' by which a thoughtful person may better understand God's power and mercy. The opening verses of chapter 16, for example, give a sensitive description of nature's bounty in the mysteries of conception, in the use of cattle, in rain, in crops, in hills, rivers and stars, and it is interspersed with declarations that all these bounties are signs for those who understand and reflect upon them. Man may learn from these signs to bless God for his bounty, and to thank him for his mercy.

> It is he who stretched out the earth and set therein firm
>   mountains and rivers,
> And of every fruit he placed there two kinds, covering
>   the day with the night.
> Surely in that there are signs for a people who reflect.
> And on the earth are tracts neighbouring each to each,
> and gardens of vines, and fields sown, and palms in pairs,
> and palms single, watered with one water; and some of
> them We (i.e. God) prefer in produce above others.
> Surely in that there are signs for a people who under-
> stand. (12)

2. *Seers and Prophets*

To be aware of God's presence within the natural universe can be a profound and continuing religious experience; it has inspired poets and artists of many religions and enabled them to enter into communion with him. But there is also a need for a more explicit form of communication, a message addressed directly to particular people in their particular circumstances.

In the traditional religions abnormal utterances of any kind are believed to be communications from one or other of the deities. Such utterances may be given in trances, whether involuntary or induced in various ways through dancing, music, or in dreams, or made after much reflection by those who exercise priestly and leadership roles within the community. (13) The earliest accounts of the Jewish prophets also tell us that they were first called 'seers', people with second sight, that they were subject to emotions of ecstasy associated perhaps with music, and that they were treated as abnormal persons. 'What did that crazy fellow want with you?' asked Jehu's fellow-officers when a member of the prophetic guilds had anointed him king in an inner room of their dining-hall. (14)

It is possible that some of these abnormal phenomena persisted in individual prophets like Ezekiel to a late period in Israel's history, but they are of less importance in most of the great prophets of the ninth to the fifth centuries BC. By then they acted mainly as God's spokesmen against the apostasy and sinfulness of their times. This was a vocation to which they were summoned by the divine call, and not of their own choosing. 'I am not the kind of prophet who prophesies for pay,' declared Amos. 'I am a herdsman and I take care of fig-trees. But the Lord took me from my work as a shepherd and ordered me to go and prophesy to his people Israel. So now listen to what the Lord says.' His experience was echoed by Isaiah who heard God's summons while worshipping in the Temple, and by Jeremiah when he saw natural objects around him invested with new and prophetic significance.

The Sovereign Lord never does anything without revealing his plan to his servants, the prophets.

When a lion roars, who can avoid being afraid?
When the Sovereign Lord speaks, who can avoid
proclaiming his message? (15)

The prophets of the Old Testament made their decisive
contribution to the development of Jewish religion through
the great crises of the Assyrian and Babylonian destruction
of Samaria and Jerusalem, the exile of the leading men
to Mesopotamia, and the subsequent rebuilding of Jerusalem and its Temple by returning exiles. They kept alive
the faith of Israel in Yahweh, the one living God, and
nourished it in response to the destruction of the Temple
and the exile of many Jews from the Promised Land.
Through their preaching, the Jewish religion developed
to recognize the universal sovereignty of the one living
God, and to appreciate the ethical nature of his rule;
infidelity and immorality, whether in personal conduct or
in public and business life, incurred his judgement. But
the prophets, and particularly Hosea and Jeremiah, also
taught God's faithful, compassionate love, which persisted
in seeking Israel's good through judgement and disaster.
Some even began to teach that God's compassion was not
for Israel only, but included other nations as well. One
of the distinctive contributions which the prophets made
was to speak of a future when God's universal rule would
be established on earth, and his righteous will obeyed
everywhere. That would be the true festival-day of the
Lord, when the Temple at Jerusalem would be set high
among the hills as a place of pilgrimage for all the nations.

The characteristic form in which the prophets preached
was to speak as if their words were a message from God
which they were charged to convey to others. They were
so convinced indeed that they were acting as God's spokes-

men that they did not hesitate to preface their words with such phrases as 'This is the word of the Lord': 'Hear the word of the Lord': 'Thus says the Lord': 'These are the words of the Lord to me'. In addition they described visions and, on occasions, were commanded to perform specific actions as signs to those who observed them. 'These are the words of the Lord: Go and buy an earthenware jar. Then take with you some of the elders of the people and of the priests, and go out to the Valley of Benhinnom ... Then you must shatter the jar before the eyes of the men who have come with you and say to them, "These are the words of the Lord of Hosts: Thus will I shatter this people and this city as one shatters an earthenware vessel so that it cannot be mended!"' (16)

But while claiming to announce God's word to their people, the Hebrew prophets did not hesitate to use the different styles familiar to their contemporaries. Their writings contain many different types of poetry, lamentations, hymns and prayers, as well as prose passages, letters, parables and sermons. (17)

On a restricted scale, there is a similar variety in the prophecies which are contained in the Qur'ān. Of all the faiths Islamic doctrine, however, developed most intensely the conviction, widespread in a variety of religions, that God uses human messengers, his prophets, to reveal his will and his word to men. It combined this with a correspondingly high view of scripture as the means of God's revelation. In the next section we shall discuss briefly the part that scriptures play in religious experience and after that consider the particular developments which have a central place in Islam.

3. *Who taught Man by the Pen what he did not know* (18)

In the Jewish scriptures, the prophets played a large part
in the history of Israel and their different prophecies gave
a coherent message. Every prophet stamped his own particular emphasis upon the messages which he gave, but
they were all united in proclaiming the sovereignty of
God and his demand for righteousness and loyalty in the
nation.

Several motives prompted the preservation of the messages of the prophets, first in oral tradition and then in
written form. The individual prophet was able to reach
a wider audience in this way, and also to secure confirmation of the truth of his preaching by preserving it for
corroboration by future events. It may even be that the
prophet whose messages were gathered into the second
part of the book named Isaiah relied mainly upon writing
for their preservation, since they were issued in Mesopotamia during a period of political upheaval when other
ways of communicating the message could have been
difficult. A prophet's disciples would also have an interest
in preserving their master's teaching, since it had touched
their hearts and claimed their loyalty.

Isaiah, for example, referred explicitly to committing
his preaching in written form to those who would preserve
it: 'Fasten up the message, seal the oracle with my teaching
[or, among my disciples]; and I will wait for the Lord.'
Jeremiah had a scribe, Baruch, who wrote his message at
Jeremiah's direction. (19) A further motive for the preservation of the prophetic messages in writing was the support
which prophets found in the preaching of those who had
preceded them; this was important, as each individual
prophet was in a vulnerable position.

There were usually several stages in the compilation of

these written documents. First the prophet himself, or his disciples, gathered his messages together into consecutive collections, much as the works of a modern poet are put together for publication at intervals. Secondly, the oral tradition was embodied in written documents following the death of the prophet or of his immediate disciples. Thirdly, other material was added to the collection of prophecies, in order to explain them or to develop their teaching further. This is how many of the longer books in the Bible reached their present form; Isaiah is a good example. (20)

Single writings reached their final forms in this way; the story of how the recognized scriptures of the major faiths, like the Christian Bible or the Hindu scriptures, have been collected together is even more complicated. Except for the Qur'ān they have all developed over a considerable period of time, and are built up of material from a number of different sources. A point, however, was always reached when a particular collection of scriptures was thought to have found its final form and no more could be added. Sometimes this point was reached in two stages and a distinction made between two groups of scriptures, one of which was considered to be of greater authority because it was closer to the source of original inspiration than the second. There is a clear distinction between two groups in Hinduism, and in the Christian Bible a similar distinction is made between the canonical books of the Old Testament and the Apocrypha. Sometimes the point of completion is marked by a change of language – there is such a change in the Old Testament between the Hebrew and the Greek writings – or it may be related to the death of the original witnesses of the prophet's or teacher's ministry; in the New Testament all the different books are associated directly or indirectly with one or other of the apostles.

Hindus distinguish between the four Vedas which are the primary scriptures and designated *śruti*, truth as it was revealed to the sages of old, and the other scriptures which are designated *smṛti*, truth remembered and handed on from generation to generation. The four books of the Veda ('Wisdom' or 'Knowledge'), have each three main sections:

> *The Mantras*: hymns and formulas used in worship of the gods; these are the oldest stratum of the whole, and may date from 1500–1000 BC, the primary collection being the Rig-Veda, the royal Veda.
> *The Brāhmaṇas*: instructions for the priests who carried out sacrifices.
> *The Upanishads*: the philosophic treatises which comment upon the sacrificial rituals.

The other scriptures, those in the *smṛti* category, include many sectarian works of philosophy as well as mythological verses extolling one or other of the great gods, and the two great epics, the *Rāmāyaṇa* and the *Mahābhārata*. The *smṛti* literature was open to all, while the *śruti* could only be read by the priests and higher castes. (21)

The core of Buddhist scriptures represent the teaching of the Buddha himself, and of the *Śrāvaka*, or 'auditors' of the Buddha, who were faithful to it. His teaching was first preserved by oral tradition, but later written records came to be made. As early as the third century BC inscriptions of the great Buddhist Emperor Aśoka (272–236 BC) recommended the monks to read them. These early scriptures were gathered together in Ceylon in the first century BC, written in Pāli, but their exact content was not fixed until later. They remain the primary scriptures of *Theravāda* Buddhism and are known as the *Three Baskets*, the *Tripiṭaka*.

The *Vinaya-piṭaka*, or Discipline Basket, contains five books of detailed regulations for the lives of monks and nuns.

The *Sutta-piṭaka*, or Sermon Basket, contains collected discourses and sayings of the Buddha. It includes the *Dhammapada*, 'Way of Truth', a collection of poetry which is the best known of all Buddhist sacred texts. (See below page 116).

The *Abhidhamma-piṭaka*, or Basket of the Supreme Dharma. These books contain the most advanced teachings of Buddhist metaphysics and were finally codified about AD 450, nearly a thousand years after the death of the Buddha.

In *Mahāyāna* Buddhism, practised in China, Korea and Japan, there is a corresponding threefold division of scriptures into *Vinaya*, or rules for religious orders, *Sūtras*, or discourses of the Buddha, and *Śāstras*, philosophical treatises by religious teachers. Other material developed over the centuries and the Chinese, Japanese and Tibetan canons of *Mahāyāna* scriptures are much more voluminous and less homogeneous than the Pāli canon. Some Buddhist scriptures survive in Sanskrit, but many of the original scriptures are now lost.

Buddhists make an important distinction between the Śāstras, or treatises written by different teachers and the Sūtras, or discourses. A sūtra is a text which it is claimed was spoken by the Buddha himself. It always begins, 'Thus I have heard at one time. The Lord dwelt at ...', and the 'I' refers to the disciple Ānanda, who recited the Buddha's words after his death. The long period of oral tradition has made it possible for many sūtras to be composed centuries after the Buddha's death. *Theravāda* Buddhists only recognize as authentic those that were recited at the first Council after the Buddha's death, at Rājagriha (in 486 BC) but *Mahāyāna* Buddhists accept sūtras composed centuries later. (22)

An important section of the Old Testament is the group of so-called historical books, from Genesis to Ezra-Nehemiah. Beginning with the myths of the creation and the sagas of the nation's founding fathers, the patriarchs, the narrative describes the long events of Israel's history from the exodus out of Egypt, through the conquest of Palestine and the establishment of Jerusalem as the Jewish capital, to the exile in Babylon and the subsequent return to the Promised Land. It is not a straightforward history; it includes different kinds of literature, sagas, folk-tales, ritual directions and law-codes, official records, and behind the written form lies the oral tradition. In the New Testament, the four Gospels and the Book of Acts are also narrative books, though they are more homogeneous than those of the Old Testament.

This emphasis upon history, the actual time and space sequence of events over long periods in the development of a single nation, is a particular characteristic of God's revelation as Jews and Christians understand it. As we shall see in the next section, it is also characteristic of Islam, although, in the Qur'ān, attention is directed in a more selective way towards a limited span of history. This attitude grows out of the belief that God is concerned and involved in the actual physical world which he has created, particularly in its human aspects, and that he is working towards the fulfilment of his purposes. Human people are responsible and free agents, and they may act contrary to the will of God; but patiently and unobtrusively God is one of the actors in the ongoing drama, and, in the long term, the dominant figure on the stage of history. History, in the biblical view, is neither dependent upon human initiative and activity nor is it a meaningless cycle of events as Hinduism and Buddhism affirm: it is the sphere where the Word of God is constantly confronting mankind through historical events and prophetic comments upon them in order to fulfil God's purposes.

The Hebrew prophets claimed that their message was a response to the promptings of God, which had come to them from outside themselves with overwhelming force and conviction. Moses was also believed to have received the Law from God to give to the people, and many of the legal enactments associated with him are prefaced by the words, 'and the Lord spoke to Moses ...' Wisdom too was recognized as a gift from God; this is symbolized in the accounts of King Solomon's wisdom and of his skill in propounding proverbs. 'When the people of Israel heard of Solomon's decision, they were all filled with deep respect for him, because they knew that God had given him the wisdom to settle disputes fairly.' 'God gave Solomon unusual wisdom and insight, and knowledge too great to be measured.' (23)

All the writings in the Bible were eventually believed to be a means of revelation and their writers were said to be inspired by the Spirit of God. This claim was made in the Old Testament, for example, in the 'last song' attributed to David: 'The spirit of the Lord speaks through me; his message is on my lips.' (24) Endorsed by Jesus, this became a standard explanation in the New Testament of the way in which the Old Testament scriptures conveyed the Word of God. St Paul described them as 'God-breathed', and elsewhere it is written: 'no one can interpret any prophecy of scripture by himself. For it was not through any human whim that men prophesied of old; men they were, but impelled by the Holy Spirit, they spoke the words of God.' (25) In their turn some writers of the New Testament scriptures believed that they also were guided by divine inspiration; Paul, for example, wrote that his 'words were taught not by human wisdom but by the Spirit', and John of Patmos ascribed his great vision to the influence of the divine Spirit upon him. Thus, when the New Testament came to take its place with the Old in the complete Bible, it was claimed that the writers of all its different books were inspired by the Spirit of God. (26)

4. *The Uncreated Qur'ān*

Islam developed within an environment similar to that in which the Bible had some centuries earlier come to be accepted as inspired scripture, and the Qur'ān, its sacred book, refers on occasions to various sections of the Bible: the Law, the Psalms, and the Gospels. But Islamic theology associated the Qur'ān absolutely with the Word of God, in a very different way from the attitudes of other religions to their scriptures.

Muhammad began to preach in Mecca, an important caravan town, in about AD 610. At the centre of the town was the sanctuary known as the *Ka'ba* and its widely acknowledged sanctity gave protection to caravans journeying to and from Mecca. Muhammad, deeply religious, felt himself called to preach to his fellow-townsmen, awakening them to their dependence upon God and their accountability to him. He expressed this message in short, vivid poems of fire and passion which continue to have a profound effect upon their hearers today. Muhammad believed that these messages were given to him by God.

Within a few years Muhammad gathered together a group of people who had responded to his preaching, and he taught them the way of Islam, namely, how to live in submission to the will of God and in dependence upon him. As various needs came to the fore in his community, Muhammad received other messages for their guidance. At the heart of his message was the affirmation of God's sole sovereignty and the rejection of all other objects of worship, including images in the Ka'ba itself.

In the year AD 622, Muhammad moved to Medina, an important oasis town three hundred miles north of Mecca. This move, the *Hijra*, was at the invitation of the Arab tribespeople in Medina, and they gave Muhammad the position of arbiter within the community. In the Muslim community, the centre of attention became, for the first time, not a sacred building or a sacred image but Muhammad as God's prophet, the message which God gave to him, and the prayer-act (*ṣalāt*), which he taught his followers.

During the remaining ten years of his life, Muhammad united most of the warring tribes of Arabia under his authority and won them over to the practice of Islam. Throughout this time, he continued to receive messages which he passed on to the community. These later Medinan messages were necessarily different from those which had been given at Mecca. They were often instructions about legal and social problems or reflections upon the recurrent crises which faced the growing Muslim community.

The messages which Muhammad received from God during the twenty-two years of his ministry in Mecca and Medina form the Qur'ān, the sacred scriptures of the Muslim community. They were gathered together by Zayd ibn Thābit, who had been Muhammad's secretary, as well as by others; a definitive edition was finally prepared by Zayd. This became the only authorized version throughout the Muslim world, and there is little doubt that it is entirely authentic.

The style of the Qur'ān indicates that its words are to be taken as the words of God or, in later passages, of his angels, and that they were addressed directly to Muhammad, either personally by way of encouragement, exhortation, rebuke, or advice, or so that he might communicate them to others. Very often what Muhammad is to say is prefixed by the word 'say'. For example: 'Say: "I am forbidden to worship what you invoke besides Allāh." Say: "I will not follow your lusts: I would then be in error and not one of those rightly guided."' (27) Sometimes the message is directly addressed to the Muslims, 'you who have believed', or to the Jews and Christians, 'People of the Book'. Detailed examination will confirm in every instance that the Qur'ān claims to be the very speech of God. Its style resembles that of the passages in the Old Testament prophets to which I referred in the previous section, and, like them, the different sections of the Qur'ān refer to particular events and circumstances.

Muhammad's assessment of his ministry and of the messages which were given to him to proclaim changed and developed during the course of his work. At first he believed that he had been entrusted with an Arabic scripture just as Moses, David and Jesus had been entrusted with other versions of the Heavenly Book, the Law, the Psalms, and the Gospel; later he believed that the Qur'ān was the final and crowning revelation of the Heavenly Book which superseded all those that preceded it. In Mecca he claimed the status of a prophet; later, in his days of power in Medina, he claimed the status of one of the (nine) apostles, only one of whom is sent to any particular people. He was then addressed as 'the Prophet' and called 'the seal [or last] of the prophets'. (28)

From first to last Muhammad was clear about two things: the Qur'ān was an objective reality which existed independently of his own mind or tongue; the Qur'ān was communicated to him by the deliberate will of God.

These two facts about Muhammad's understanding of the nature of the Qur'ān are supported by details in Muslim accounts of the prophet's life:

1. Muhammad was reluctant to begin his ministry and only did so vigorously when he had been given, for a second time, the vision of an angel (or God himself) 'sitting on a throne between heaven and earth'.

> Your comrade is not astray, neither errs, nor speaks out of caprice.
> This is nothing but a revelation revealed, which one terrible in power, very strong, taught him.
> He stood poised, being on the higher horizon, then drew near and suspended hung, two bows'-length away, or nearer; then he revealed to his servant what he revealed.
> His heart does not lie about what he saw. (29)

The first vision in which he heard the divine call to be

a prophet had in fact caused Muhammad considerable distress.

2. The words associated with the vision which called him to prophesy emphasized his duty to transmit the message committed to him.

> You who are clothed in your mantle,
> Get up and warn,
> Declare the greatness of your Lord,
> Purify your garments,
> Flee from defilement (or idolatry);
> Do not bestow favours in order to gain more,
> But be patiently steadfast towards your Lord. (30)

This emphasis remained clear in Muhammad's preaching throughout his ministry. 'Obey God and obey [God's] apostle. If you turn away (from the message), he must carry what is laid upon him and you what has been laid upon you. If you obey him, you will be rightly guided. The apostle's only responsibility is to deliver the clear message.' (31)

3. Muhammad distinguished all through his life between those messages which were given to him to become part of the Qur'ān, and all his other pronouncements, decisions and addresses.

4. Muhammad's reception of the messages which he was given to form part of the Qur'ān was associated with physical sensations. In particular, he appears to have experienced strong inner tension, sometimes marked by feelings of cold, perspiration and sensations of bright lights: 'Revelation,' said his wife 'Ā'isha, 'used to come to him like the breaking of the dawn.' These sensations are well attested and appear to have continued all through his

life, and they are similar to the experiences of other prophets, in the Old Testament and elsewhere.

Traditionally, the first passage of the Qur'ān to be revealed to Muhammad is the following:

Recite (*iqra'*) in the name of your Lord who created.
He created Man from a blood-clot.
Recite: your Lord is the Most Generous,
Who taught by the pen;
He taught Man what he did not know.
No indeed: Man waxes insolent:
he thinks himself independent,
But to your Lord he returns (for judgement). (32)

Muslim scholars infer the priority of this revelation from its use of the word 'recite', which comes from the same root as *al-Qur'ān*, 'the recitation'. The verb *qara'a* can mean 'to read', but this is a later usage and most frequently in the Qur'ān its meaning is the older one 'to recite or to proclaim'. In Syriac writings (linked with Arabic but of an earlier period), *qeryānā* is used for the scripture readings read in church. (33)

This illustrates clearly what was intended from the beginning of Muhammad's ministry; in teaching his followers the way of prayer and worship, he was giving to them inspired scriptures for recitation in worship, similar to those used by contemporary Jews and Christians.

Orthodox Muslim doctrine about the Qur'ān was formulated during the first three centuries and has changed very little since then. However, as in Christianity, there was intense and bitter controversy during this early period, similar to the controversies in Christianity about the relationship between Christ and God. It was easy enough to assert that the Qur'ān was a message from God, but difficult to define its precise relationship with him. (34)

Abū Ḥanīfa, a theologian who died in AD 767, stated the orthodox Muslim belief about the Qur'ān as follows: 'The Qur'ān is the speech of Allāh, written in the copies, preserved in the memories, recited by the tongues, revealed to the Prophet. Our pronouncing, writing and reciting the Qur'ān is created, whereas the Qur'ān itself is uncreated.' (35) A modern confession of faith, written by a father in prison to his son, put it like this: 'I believe that the Holy Koran descended on Muhammad, prayer and peace be on him, and that it contains all the fundamental principles which Islam brought, whether they be of faith, rituals, social system, or morality. Although the great Koran descended in the tongue of the Arabs, addressing them in their own language and in their own mentality of that age, it contains moral and spiritual principles for man everywhere and in every age ... It is truly Allah's book, and it is the miracle of the illiterate prophet: men of literature, rhetoric and wisdom fail to equal it in part or in full.' (36)

Thus, for Muslims, the Qur'ān is a miraculous intrusion, or series of intrusions, into human life through the person of the Prophet, which cannot be repeated. Its very language, Arabic, is important. Muslims say that when the Qur'ān is translated into another language it ceases to be the Qur'ān, and almost all the authorities insist that the Qur'ān must be recited in Arabic during the prayers. The only exception is the Ḥanafī school which permits the use of other languages if the person concerned is unable to recite it in Arabic. Originally Abū Ḥanīfa himself permitted the use of translation and this suggests that he may have recognized the Qur'ān to be the *meaning* rather than the language of the Arabic text. (37) This was the teaching of al-Ghazzālī, one of the greatest theologians of Islam (died AD 1111), who wrote: 'the words of the Qur'ān belong to the world in which we live, their meanings belong to the "world of the angels". The Qur'ān is divine in its origin and is revealed to those who possess a God-given faculty of intuition beyond the plane of intelligence.' The Ṣūfī mystics also spoke of an 'outer' and an 'inner' meaning in the Qur'ān and allegorized many of its supernatural features.

The last two hundred years, however, have exposed the Islamic world to all kinds of new pressures – those associated with science and technology, communications and development, pluralism and the growth of secular philosophies and political systems. In common with other religions, Islam is being deeply and seriously influenced by these developments, and traditional theology questioned. Muslims have responded to these pressures in several different ways.

Some defend traditional orthodoxy. For them the Qur'ān is a symbol, the core of a traditional culture which must be defended at all costs. Others have welcomed a modern emphasis upon literary study of the language and style of the Qur'ān, and there are a growing number of studies of this kind, especially in Egypt. (38) Others, particularly Muslim thinkers in India-Pakistan, have sought to draw out from the Qur'ān what they regard as the essential principles of Islam, with a consequent depreciation of the historical context of particular passages and Qur'ānic themes. Each reconstruction is different and I give a single example from the work of Asaf Fyzee, a distinguished Muslim lawyer in India. 'To me it is clear that we cannot go "back" to the Qur'an, we have to go "forward" with it. I wish to *understand* the Qur'an as it was understood by the Arabs of the time of the Prophet only to *reinterpret* it and apply it to my conditions of life and to believe in it, so far as it appeals to me as a twentieth-century man. I cannot be called upon to live in the desert, to traverse it on camel-back, to eat locusts, to indulge in vendetta, to wear a beard and a cloak, and to cultivate a pseudo-Arab mentality. I must distinguish between poetic truth and factual truth. I must distinguish between the husk and the kernel of religion, between law and legend.

'I believe that the Qur'an is a message from God. It is the voice of God heard by Muhammad ... God spoke to him and he spoke to us. The Qur'an is a testimony of his faith in God. Muhammad was a man like us; but the word was the Word of God.' (39)

5. *The Word became a Human Being*

Christians share with other religions the belief that God reveals himself in a general way through the natural universe, and, in a more particular way, through the prophets and the scriptures which transmit their words to succeeding generations. Many Christians indeed have a very high view of the authority of the scriptures contained in the Bible, and do not hesitate to speak about them as 'the Word of God'. This usage is founded on passages in the New Testament which emphasize the close link between the scriptures and the Holy Spirit who is believed to have inspired their writers. But Christian reverence for the Bible as a means by which God reveals his nature and will to men is always secondary to the belief that Jesus has made God known to men in a unique way, and that he has done so not only by his words, but by his whole life and his person. 'No one has ever seen God. The only Son, who is the same as God and is at the Father's side, he has made him known.' (40)

Jesus proclaimed the kingly rule of God and declared the over-riding importance of his kingdom; even more he demonstrated the presence and nature of that kingdom by the quality of his life. He knew that he himself had been called to set forward God's kingdom and, in obedience to this calling, he accepted that there was a direct and special relationship between himself and God whose kingdom he proclaimed. This relationship was integral to his ministry; it was of a piece with his understanding of his mission and reflected the impression which he made on his friends and disciples. The Greek theologians coined a word to express the identification of Jesus with God's kingdom: they spoke of him in a single Greek word, *autobasileia*, as 'the very kingdom itself'.

That the relationship between Jesus and God was a central feature of his ministry is shown in three particular ways. First, in his private prayers, he spoke directly to God using the word with which small children addressed their fathers in Palestinian homes; it expressed Jesus' complete dependence upon God, and his use of the Aramaic word *'abbā* was so characteristic a feature of his prayers that his disciples used it when describing them, even when they were talking or writing in Greek. (41) Secondly, he did not hesitate to invite people to become his disciples, and to follow him with complete loyalty. 'Whoever comes to me,' he said, 'cannot be my disciple unless he loves me more than he loves his father and his mother, his wife and his children, his brothers and his sisters, and himself as well. Whoever does not carry his own cross [the symbol of death], and come after me cannot

be my disciple.' And, thirdly, he claimed to reveal God
to men in such a way that to reject his message was
equivalent to rejecting God himself: 'My Father,' he said,
'has given me all things. No one knows who the Son is
except the Father, and no one knows who the Father is
except the Son and those to whom the Son chooses to reveal
him . . . whoever welcomes me, also welcomes the one who
sent me . . . and whoever rejects me rejects the one who
sent me.' It is significant that these words occur in the
Synoptic Gospels, those of Matthew, Mark and Luke,
which pass on to us most directly the traditions of Jesus'
ministry. (42)

During his earthly life, Jesus' disciples thought of him
as a man who had been specially chosen by God. Although
'*rabbi*' (teacher) and 'prophet' were the titles most
commonly given to him by his contemporaries, his closest
disciples became convinced, at a crucial stage in his
ministry, that he was the chosen 'Messiah', God's envoy,
whose coming had been predicted by the prophets.
Towards the end of his ministry Jesus publicly accepted
the role of the Messiah of Peace when he rode at the head
of the pilgrims into Jerusalem. According to the Gospel
narratives, his disciples gave him other titles, including
'Son of God', but on the one hand 'Son of God' sometimes
meant little more than the word 'Messiah', of which it
could serve as a synonym, and, on the other hand, the
Gospel narratives reflect at times the later usage of the
churches after his passion and resurrection. This is particularly true of the Gospel of John, which was probably
written in old age by a disciple who had spent many years
telling the story of Jesus to Greek-speaking people in Asia
Minor. 'Prophet', 'Messiah', perhaps 'Son of God', were
as far as Jesus' disciples could go in affirming his close

relationship with God at a time when he was still living a natural human life amongst them. (43)

This was changed by events after the death of Jesus on the cross in Jerusalem. On the second day he came to his disciples and they knew that he was alive. They believed that God had raised him from the dead, and this was confirmed to them when he came in visible form to different members of their group on several occasions during a period of forty days. On the last occasions that he met with them in this way he commissioned them to take his message to the whole world; after that they never saw him in the same way again. They believed that he had 'ascended into heaven', to share in the authority and power of God. Shortly after this, when they met together in prayer, they felt themselves inspired and strengthened in a new way by the Spirit of God, and they began the task of telling the 'good news of Jesus' to the whole world. (44)

In telling their story, the first Christians found themselves having to answer the question: 'Who is Jesus?' Christians have answered this in a number of different ways; in one sense no final answer can ever be given, since all attempts to give one grow out of worship and express the affirmations of faith. But the attempts have two things in common; first, they try to define both the relationship between Jesus and God and that between Jesus and other people; secondly, they all refer back to the statements which are made about him in the scriptures of the New Testament, statements which represent the beliefs and practice of the Christian churches during the first century AD.

The earliest tradition shows that the believers thought of Jesus as the one who had been chosen by God to be the saviour of mankind, and who had, after the crucifixion, been vindicated by the resurrection and exalted to share in God's power and glory; they also expected that he would return as judge on the day of judgement. According to Acts 1–10, they referred to him by a title, 'the Servant', which had been used of certain prophets and of Israel herself in the Old Testament, and by others also which contemporary Jewish writers gave to the hoped-for Messiah; 'Lord', 'the Holy One', 'the Just One', 'the Prince', 'the Saviour', 'the Judge'. Later books in the New Testament reflect this way of thinking, though with significant developments.

The use of the title 'Messiah', or its Greek equivalent 'Christ', was, however, linked with two other titles which Christians used in order to emphasize the close relationship of Jesus with God. 'Lord' (*kurios*) was one of these, and it was used as a title for the Roman emperors to whom divine honours were paid, and also for some Greek deities; it had, however, even closer association in Christian circles with the Greek translation of the Old Testament in which it was used as the equivalent of the Hebrew, Yahweh, the proper name for God. In Christian usage this title affirmed Christ's divinity without asserting his identity with God, and it had many shades of meaning. The formula used first as a declaration of Christian faith by converts at their baptism were the simple words, 'Jesus is Lord'. (45) The other title, 'Son of God' was used occasionally as a synonym for 'Messiah', sometimes even for kings of Israel who were anointed with sacred oil as God's vice-regents. Paul, for example, the most influential of the apostles in developing the Church's theology, is said in Acts to have used 'Son of God' and 'Messiah' almost as synonyms when he first became a Christian, and this reflects Jewish usage. (46)

The title 'Son of God' was of rich significance and was developed by the first Christian theologians in a variety of ways. Paul, for example, developed it to include the idea of the pre-existence of the Son in the life of the Godhead before his incarnation in Jesus of Nazareth, and to affirm that he had been the agent of God in the creation of the universe. 'Christ is the visible likeness of the invisible God. He is the first-born Son, superior to all created things. For through him God created everything in heaven and on earth ... God created the whole universe through him and for him. Christ existed before all things, and in union with him all things have their proper place.' The unknown author of the Letter to the Hebrews also used the title 'Son' to emphasize the unique and abiding relationship between God and the Messiah. His words take up the theme of God's Word: 'When in former times God spoke to our forefathers, he spoke in fragmentary and varied fashion through the prophets. But in this final age he has spoken to us through his Son, whom he has made heir to the whole universe, and through whom he created all orders of existence: the Son is the effulgence of God's splendour and the stamp of God's very being, and sustains the universe by his word of power. When he had brought about the cleansing of sins, he took his seat at the right hand of the Majesty on high, raised as far above the angels as the title he had inherited is superior to theirs.' (47)

The title 'Son of God', however, with its Messianic associations, was inadequate to carry all the meaning which Christians wished to express through it, and, as the Qur'ān shows, it is a term liable to misunderstanding. (48) The apostles, therefore, went on to use Jewish and Greek concepts about the creation of the world to express the unique and eternal relationship between Christ and God.

Centuries before, the Hebrew prophets had emphasized
God's creative activity in their preaching, and the following passage from Jeremiah is typical:

> God made the earth by his power,
> Fixed the world by his wisdom,
> Unfurled the skies by his understanding,
> At the thunder of his voice the waters in heaven
>   roar. (49)

This passage illustrates the two ways in which Hebrew
and Jewish thinkers spoke about God's creative power.
The older tradition emphasized the divine Word as the
authoritative revelation of God's will which brought the
world into being. This is the recurrent theme of the
creation poem in the first chapter of the Bible: each successive phase in creation emerged in response to God's
sovereign word – 'God said, "Let there be light", and light
came to be.' Hebrew thinking is very close to the Qur'ānic
statement: 'The matter of it is this: when he wills a thing,
he says to it, "Be", and it comes to be.' Later developments, in the Jewish Wisdom literature, spoke of Wisdom
as a quasi-personal divine power which had emanated from
God before the creation of the material universe and was
his agent in the creation of the world. (50) This idea is
not so central in Jewish thought as is that of the Word,
but it found echoes in Greek philosophy.

Both these concepts, Word and Wisdom, are represented
in the following passage, the last stage, in the New Testament, of the search for an answer to the question 'Who
is Jesus?' 'Before the world was created, the Word already
existed; he was with God, and he was the same as God.
From the very beginning the Word was with God.

Through him God made all things; not one thing in all creation was made without him. The Word was the source of life, and this life brought light to mankind . . . The Word became a human being and, full of grace and truth, lived among us. We saw his glory, the glory which he received as the Father's only Son . . . No one has ever seen God. The only Son, who is the same as God and is at the Father's side, he has made him known.' (51) Although this statement is based on Jewish ideas, it reflects also insights of contemporary Greek thought, especially in its use of the Greek word *logos* for Word. The Greek philosophers understood by *logos*, in the sense of 'reason', a timeless and ordered pattern of beauty and truth, inherent within the whole universe and underlying its changing phenomena.

The successive stages through which Christian belief passed show how difficult it was for Christians, who were heirs to Jewish beliefs about the transcendent sovereignty of God as Creator, to define this relationship satisfactorily. Christians were wrestling with the problem of explaining to themselves and to others the unique authority of Jesus and his immediate access to the mind and will of God. The effect of Jesus upon Christians, however, was not dependent only upon what his disciples remembered of the life which he had lived with them during his earthly ministry. Even after the resurrection and ascension, Christians believed him to be alive in their midst, and especially in their services of worship and of Holy Communion. So Christians do until today, and this makes the question 'Who is Jesus?' as much a contemporary one as it was in earlier centuries. It is concerned with explaining adequately and intelligibly the fact that Jesus, whether as known through the written Gospels, or through the life of the Church, communicates the presence of God in a direct and unprecedented way to those who respond to him in trust and love.

Throughout history the churches have authorized statements of their beliefs about the relationship between Christ and God, and with the Holy Spirit. These beliefs cannot be verified by argument or by demonstration; they are grounded in religious experience alone, the experience both of those who make them and of past generations gathered up into the tradition of the whole Church. This does not imply that they may not be questioned but rather that they must be verified afresh by each new generation of believers, in the reality of their own experience. It is inevitable, therefore, that the beliefs themselves should be subject to constant restatement and reinterpretation.

Christians share with other religions the belief that God has revealed himself, his mind and will, to his creatures in many different ways: through the natural universe which he created, through prophets, poets and artists, through inspired scriptures and through communion with him in prayer. But they also believe that God revealed himself by the incarnation of his Word, once and for all, in Jesus of Nazareth. They believe that by this act God became man, and entered into the reality of human existence in a way which allows no withdrawal. The destiny of humanity is inextricably bound up with the destiny of the whole creation, and, beyond that, with the destiny of God himself. (52)

Postscript

God's will and nature are revealed to his creatures in a variety of ways. Through the mysteries and forces of the natural universe they come to know the transcendent being who is the ground of its existence and the source of its life. In the Semitic religions, this led to an affirmation of the sole sovereignty of God.

The transcendent is heard to speak in more specific ways as well. Prophets and other teachers were accepted as God's living messengers and their messages reproduced in the scriptures of the several religions; their words become of universal significance through the books which record them. This process reached its climax in Islam in which the Qur'ān is identified with the uncreated Word of God. In contrast with other religions, Christians identify God's Word in a unique and final way with a single person, Jesus Christ, in the totality of his life and teaching; prophets and scriptures, although important means of revelation, are only secondary.

Potentially, Word is divisive; in particular, the claims made by Christianity and Islam in respect of Jesus and the Qur'ān can create a lack of sympathy between Christians and Muslims and also towards the claims of others to have heard the word of God addressed to them. More generally, the loyalty which communities give to their own scriptures, beliefs, ways and places of worship, linked as they are with particular cultural and historical associations, can cause mistrust and antagonism towards others.

These particular claims can only be reconciled with great difficulty and through determined efforts to achieve mutual understanding. Any such efforts must take into account the following considerations.

'Words', though unique and accepted by those who hear them as revelations of the transcendent, are spoken in particular contexts and with reference to particular events. Although revelations of what is infinite and eternal, they are themselves historically conditioned.

There is consensus between the religions of the Old and New Testaments and the Qur'ān, that the one eternal God makes himself known through the natural universe of which he is the Creator. At first sight this is in conflict with the apparent polytheism of some traditional religions and with Vedic Hinduism in which deities are closely associated with particular natural phenomena. Yet one attitude is common to both, namely belief that the natural universe is a medium through which man enters into a relationship with God.

There are many similarities between the responses of dependent trust, of worship, and moral behaviour which the Word evokes from those who hear it in different ways within particular communities. These responses form the shape of religious experience at the level of everyday life, and there is much common ground between the religions.

The transcendent can never be fully comprehended by human creatures whose lives are limited by the constraints of their physical existence and marked by imperfection and death. The Ground of all Being transcends all thoughts or speech about him.

NOTES

1. A. C. Bouquet, *Hinduism*, 30–31. R. C. Zaehner, *Hinduism*, 29, suggests that other deities are anthropomorphic representations of moral concepts and cites *Mitra*, 'the compact', and perhaps *Varuṇa*, 'the oath'.
2. *Hindu Scriptures*, (R. C. Zaehner), 3.
3. Bouquet, op. cit., 29.

4. Zaehner, *Hindu Scriptures*, vi.

5. See Zaehner, op. cit., 14–35 and Bouquet, 26–36.

6. See *A Guide to Religions*, chapter 3, and G. Lienhardt, op. cit.

7. See chapters 4, 5 and 6 in *A Guide to Religions*: also E. G. Parrinder, *African Traditional Religions*, London, SPCK, 1968.

8. e.g. Qur'ān 17, 22–3 and 39.

9. Isaiah 45. 11–19: 40. 18–19, 25: Q.73. 8–9.

10. Psalm 19. 1; Amos 4. 13 (NEB); Isaiah 40.

11. Gerhard von Rad, *Wisdom in Israel*, SCM, 1972, chapter IX: Matthew 5. 43–8 and 6. 25–34.

12. Q. 13. 3–4.

13. See J. Taylor, *The Primal Vision*, chapter 10.

14. 2 Kings 9. 11: see also 1 Samuel 9. 1–14: 10. 5–6.

15. Amos 7. 14–16: Isaiah 6: Jeremiah 1: Amos 3. 7–8.

16. Jeremiah 19. 1–14 (NEB).

17. See J. Lindblom, *Prophecy in Ancient Israel*, Oxford, Blackwell, 1963, 155.

18. Q. 96. 4–5.

19. See Isaiah 8. 16 (NEB): Jeremiah 36 and 45.

20. Cf. e.g. C. Westermann, *Handbook to the Old Testament*, SPCK, 1969, 135–54.

21. See Bouquet, *Hinduism*, 26–8; Zaehner, *Hinduism*, 9–12: T. K. Thomas, in *A Guide to Religions*, 64–5.

22. See Conze, op. cit., 28–34; Lamotte, op. cit., vol. I, 34–7; Lynn de Silva, in *A Guide to Religions*, 137–39.

23. See Exodus 19 and 24: I Kings 3. 4–28 and 4. 29–34.

24. 2 Samuel 23. 2.

25. Mark 12. 36: 2 Timothy 3. 16: 2 Peter 1. 20–21 (NEB).

26. 1 Corinthians 2. 13: Revelation 1. 10.

27. Q. 6. 56.

28. See R. Bell, *Introduction to the Qur'ān*, Edinburgh, 1953, chapter 7.
29. Q. 53. 1–11.
30. Q. 74. 1–7.
31. Q. 24. 54.
32. Q. 96. 1–8.
33. A. Jeffery, *The Foreign Vocabulary of the Qur'ān*, Baroda, 1938, 234.
34. See D. B. Macdonald, *The Development of Muslim Theology*, etc., London, 1926, part iii; A. J. Wensinck, *The Muslim Creed*, Cambridge, 1932: *Shorter Encyclopaedia of Islam*, 'al-Mu'tazila'.
35. R. Bell. op. cit., 37.
36. Mohammed Fadhel Jamali, *Letters on Islam*, London, 1978, 38–9.
37. See A. L. Tibāwī, 'Is the Qur'ān translatable?', in *Muslim World*, 1962, 4–16.
38. See Kenneth Cragg, *The Mind of the Qur'ān*, London, Allen & Unwin, 1973, chapter 1: J. M. S. Baljon, *Modern Muslim Koran Interpretation* (1880–1960), Leiden, 1968, chapter III.
39. Asaf Fyzee, *A Modern Approach to Islam*, Bombay, 1963, 94 and 109–10.
40. John 1. 18.
41. Mark 14. 36: Romans 8. 15: Galatians 4. 6.
42. Luke 14. 26–27: Mark 1. 14–20 and 2. 13–14: Luke 9. 48 and 10. 16 and 22.
43. Luke 4. 23–4: Matthew 21. 11: Luke 24. 19: Mark 8. 27–9. 1: 11. 1–11 and 15–19 with parallels. The whole development is difficult to set out in the space available here, and the reader is referred to the standard Introductions to the Gospels and the New Testament. I

have set out developments within the New Testament in my *Jesus and God*, Sheldon Press, 1967.

44. See Matthew 28, Mark 16, Luke 24, John 20–21, and Acts 1.

45. See Romans 10. 9: Philippians 2. 11.

46. Compare Acts 9. 20 and 9. 22: also Mark 14. 61: John 1. 49. For the use of the title 'Son of God' by the Hebrew kings in Jerusalem see e.g. 2 Samuel 7. 12–16: Psalm 89. 19–21 and 26–27. *Māshīaḥ, christos*, means 'anointed with oil'.

47. Colossians 1. 15–17; some scholars question whether Paul himself wrote this letter, but compare a similar statement of Christ's pre-existence in Paul's letter to the Philippians 2. 6–11, which he may have taken from a contemporary Christian hymn. Hebrews 1. 1–4 (NEB adapted).

48. Q. 19. 90–91.

49. Jeremiah 10. 12–13 (NEB adapted).

50. Genesis 1: Q. 36. 82: Proverbs 8, and Ecclesiasticus 24. 3–6 and 9. See von Rad, op. cit., 144–57.

51. John 1. 1–18. See also 1 John 1. 1–3.

52. See J. F. Bethune-Baker, *An Introduction to the Early History of Christian Doctrine*, repr. London, 1962; L. Hodgson, *The Doctrine of the Trinity*, Nisbet, 1964; David Brown, *The Divine Trinity*, Sheldon Press, 1969.

CHAPTER 4

Way

If Word is a central theme in religious experience, so also is Way. We need a pattern of conduct, a way of life to guide us in our actions and relationships, both within the families and in the wider community; the common accept-ance of a basic way of life is an indispensable condition for community. Most people express their religious faith in what they do, rather than what they believe, in terms of life-style rather than of creed. Jesus called his disciples to follow him and the first Christians were known as 'those who belong to the [Jesus] way'; the obligation to follow a particular way of life is central to Judaism and Islam as well as to Buddhism.

In all these except Buddhism the authority of each particular Way is closely linked with the word of God from which it is derived; in Buddhism the Eightfold path is associated with the Buddha's teaching and his authority as embodying the Buddha-nature. In China, however, the two classic teachings of Confucius and Tao are based on providence and good sense; they derive from an awareness of the inner nature of things, and not from any kind of supernatural or divine authority.

1. *Virtue and Simplicity*

Guidance for conduct has in China been traditionally found in the teachings of Confucius or in those of the

Taoist philosophers. (1) Despite their differences, they encourage an attitude towards life which has moulded the Chinese people, and still has influence today.

Confucius was a teacher, rather than an innovator. Born in 551 BC, he came from a poor family and spent his life as a government official. With his disciples, he revised and edited the writings of earlier Chinese philosophers and teachers; these are known as the *Five Classics*. At a much later period, the *Four Books* were set alongside them: they include the *Analects*, a collection of the sayings of Confucius made by his disciples, and the *Mencius*, the comments made on his teaching by Mencius (371–298 BC).

After his death, the local prince erected a temple in his honour, and much later this practice became common all over China. Confucius was given the title of Supreme Saint, and offerings of incense and other gifts in honour of his memory were made at annual ceremonies. This was an extension of the worship offered to the ancestors, and in Confucian temples the memorial tablets of his four associates and other scholars were placed by the side of that of Confucius. His works were the basis for the examination of officials for nearly two thousand years.

In the period when Confucius and the early Taoists developed their teaching, religion in China was already made up of its traditional three main strands: animistic beliefs associated with agriculture, veneration of the ancestors, and worship directed towards 'Heaven'. 'Heaven' was believed to possess attributes of majesty, omnipotence, intelligence and providence, and was associated with *Chang Ti*, the Most High, who was thought of as a personal God. Confucius accepted the worship of 'Heaven', as he did the cult of the ancestors, and he taught that Heaven was the power on which everything depends. (2)

The Emperor was regarded as the 'Son of Heaven', and in the conduct of everyday business the Emperor ascertained the will of Heaven by consulting the soothsayers and diviners. He also made an annual sacrifice to Heaven, thus rendering the homage which a son was bound to offer to his father. These practices also were accepted by Confucius who taught that the father-son relationship is the foundation of all human community. The son's duty is to pay proper respect to his father by caring for his parents as well as for his children, and by remembering his parents after their death by making appropriate offerings. The other relationships in life, between ruler and subject, husband and wife, older and younger, friend and friend, grow out of this fundamental relationship. (3)

Confucius, however, taught primarily about behaviour in the present world, and he asked, 'While you are not able to serve men, how can you serve their spirits? While you do not know life, how can you know about death?' His main concern was to educate the scholars who had authority in the state. The goal of life, he taught, is to discover 'the way of cultivating the self, managing one's household, governing the nation, and establishing world peace'. To do this a person must practise the five virtues, benevolence, righteousness, propriety, wisdom and trustworthiness, all of which issue in good actions. Of these five virtues, benevolence is the greatest and it is defined by Confucius in different passages of the Analects as 'to treat people as though we were attending a high sacrifice; not to do to others what we would not that they should do to us; to breed no wrongs in the state and breed no wrongs in the home': 'to love mankind': 'the practice of politeness, liberality, good faith, diligence and generosity – being polite you will not be slighted; being liberal you will win the people; having good faith you will be trusted by others; having diligence you will be successful; being generous, you will be worthy to employ others'. Confucian teaching, as it developed, taught that the five virtues are part of human nature, and derived from the principle which governs the whole universe. Evil, on the other hand, is due either to environment or to education, and unenlightened people fail to allow their true nature to appear because of their own individual character. People should return, therefore, to their true nature and purify themselves through study of right conduct, particularly as set out in the *Great Learning*, one of the *Four Books*. 'The supreme good of Man is not pleasure, nor honours, nor riches, but virtue, the source of true happiness; and virtue is attained by strength of will, firmness of purpose, moral energy in the observance of moral standards ... Man must be a sensible person who saves and beautifies himself by adapting himself imperceptibly, harmoniously, to the world in which he takes his proper place and so achieves his aims.' To quote from the *Four Books*: 'The life of the moral man is an image and a reflection of the universal order ... If the life of the moral man is such, it is because he never ceases to cultivate his moral being.' 'To be faithful to its true nature, is the law of Heaven; to strive to be so is the law of Man.' (4)

Confucianism was concerned with the education and conduct of human people in accordance with the nobility and dignity of human nature. Taoism sought to help people live in accordance with Tao, 'the Way' of the universe from which all things come. The Tao, or 'Creative Principle of the Universe', is simplicity itself, the quiet undifferentiated Ground of all Being on which all things depend. Wise men and public servants, therefore, should reflect this serene simplicity in all they do. 'The *Lao Tzu* [i.e. the *Tao Te Ching*] is, through and through, a work on the art of government ... Knowledge of the Tao makes the sage a good ruler because the government of the people should be modelled on the way the myriad creatures in the universe are ruled by the Tao,' i.e. quietly and without ostentatious effort. (5)

Heaven is eternal, the Earth everlasting.
How come they to be so? It is because they do not foster
   their own lives;
That is why they live so long.
Therefore the Sage
Puts himself in the background; but is always to the
   fore.
Remains outside but is always there.
Is it not just because he does not strive for any personal
   end
That all his personal ends are fulfilled? (6)

He who by *Tao* purposes to help a ruler of men
will oppose all conquest by force of arms;
For such things are wont to rebound.
Where armies have encamped, thorns and brambles
   grow.
The raising of a great host
Is followed by a year of dearth.
Therefore a good general effects his purpose and then
stops; he does not take further advantage of his victory.
Fulfils his purpose and does not glory in what he has
   done; ...
Fulfils his purpose, but only as a step that could not
   be avoided;

Fulfils his purpose, but without violence;
For what has a time of vigour also has a time of decay.
This is against Tao,
And what is against Tao will soon perish. (7)

At the level of ordinary morality, Taoism in its popular
form teaches Five Precepts (not to kill, drink alcohol, tell
lies, steal or to commit adultery), and Ten Virtues: filial
piety, loyalty to emperors and teachers, kindness to all
creatures, patience and reproof of wrongdoing, self-
sacrifice so as to be able to help the poor, liberating slaves
and planting trees, digging wells and making roads, teaching the ignorant and promoting welfare, studying the
scriptures and making proper offerings to the gods.

At first sight, the Taoist attitude towards life appears
to be a negative one:

Stretch a bow to the very full,
And you will wish you had stopped in time;
Temper a sword-edge to its very sharpest,
And you will find it soon grows dull.
When bronze and jade fill your hall
It can no longer be guarded.
Wealth and place breed insolence
That brings ruin in its train.
When your work is done, then withdraw!
Such is Heaven's Way. (8)

In some ways, this advice was practical in that it showed
how best to survive in the turbulent times in which the
anthology was compiled. But the passive attitude towards
life is not negative; it reflects the quietness of Tao, the
fundamental principle underlying the universe, and thus

its strength. By holding firmly to the principles of simplicity and serenity exhibited by the Tao, a ruler can transform and uplift the people.

> The more taboos there are in the empire
> The poorer the people;
> The more sharpened tools the people have
> The more benighted the state;
> The more skills the people have
> The further novelties multiply;
> The better known the laws and edicts
> The more thieves and robbers there are.

Hence the Sage says,

> I take no action and the people are transformed of themselves;
> I prefer stillness and the people are rectified of themselves;
> I am not meddlesome and the people prosper of themselves;
> I am free from desire and the people themselves become simple like the uncarved block. (9)

One with Tao, he who follows its precepts is also at one with the Ground of the Universe and with the Power associated with it, and thus achieves contentment and happiness.

> One who pursues the Way (i.e. Tao) becomes one with the Way;
> One who pursues the Power, becomes one with the Power;

One who pursues Nature, becomes one with Nature.
Being one with the Way, he is congenial to the Way,
    consequently he takes delight in the Way.
Being one with the Power, he is congenial to the Power,
    consequently he takes delight in the Power.
Being one with Nature, he is congenial to Nature,
    consequently he takes delight in Nature. (10)

There is an echo here of the teaching in the Upanishads that human happiness depends upon the attainment of communion between the individual soul and the eternal reality which is the one source of the universe in all its manifold diversity. In China this longing was expressed in terms of practical behaviour; in other cultures it has been a motive for intense mystical prayer. (11)

2. *The Eightfold Path*

In the Four Noble Truths, the Buddha taught that man's salvation lies in freeing himself from the passions and desires which are the cause of suffering, and thus attaining Nirvāna. (12) The Noble Eightfold Path taught by the Buddha shows how this may be done.

As far as *behaviour* is concerned, the disciple must practise:

Right speech: abstaining from untruthfulness, slander, harsh language and idle talk.
Right action: abstaining from killing other living creatures, from theft and sexual misconduct.
Right livelihood: earning a livelihood in a way not harmful to any living being.

But right behaviour is of no value unless the mind is trained to be free from passion. Thus the disciple is urged to purify his thoughts by efforts of *concentration*:

Right effort: avoiding evil thoughts and overcoming them, arousing good thoughts and maintaining them. The Buddhist disciple is to 'cherish in his heart boundless goodwill to all that lives'.

Right mindfulness: paying careful, watchful attention to every state of the body, feeling and mind, and disciplining them correctly.

Right concentration: reducing the activity of his thoughts, the disciple learns to concentrate on a single object, and thus to reach a state of spiritual awareness in which perception of the sentient world plays little part. He begins to make contact with the unconditioned world of Nirvāna.

Together with right action, and the mastery and purification of mental processes, goes the right *thinking* appropriate to them:

Right views: gaining an understanding of the Four Truths taught by the Buddha, and of the teaching associated with them.

Right intentions: thinking thoughts which are free from ill-will, lust, cruelty, and untruthfulness. (13)

The Dharma (Truth, Law), which is expressed in the Eightfold Path and the Four Truths, commands the Buddhist's deepest loyalty. The Buddha himself found no satisfactory answer to his quest for an absolute and transcendent reality to which he might offer veneration and respect, and so he decided to 'attach himself to the Dharma which he had himself discovered in order to honour, respect and serve it'. He declared it independent of everyone, himself included, and thus as in some sense transcendent and eternal. 'I have not created the Dharma and another has not created it either.'

Christmas Humphreys, who has done much to set Buddhism in a western context, explains the position which the Dharma holds in his religion. 'The name of my God is Dharma. What does the word mean? Its basic meaning is to sustain. Other English terms are Law, Norm, Duty, Teaching. For me my God provides a platform which sustains me; he gives meaning to life, and the purpose and agenda for this life; also the means to cope with this agenda and the power to achieve it ...

'What are the needs of Dharma, the demands of my God? Perpetual concentration on the job in hand, akin to the discipline of "right-mindfulness". Then "guts" – I know no prettier term for what I mean, the developed will to dominate the demands of self when they interfere, to walk on and walk on though the Way be dark or difficult or dull ... Thus Dharma is my companion and guide, and the means which is itself the end. He is like the carrot on the donkey's nose, the ever receding ideal, the light on the summit of Everest, the welcome on the doorstep of "my Father's home" ... For these few – and they will ever be the few – the goal is to be so one with Dharma that the self is gone. For these there will be meaning in the words – "Remain unselfish to the endless end." (14)

The essence of the Buddhist way is expressed very clearly in the 423 sayings which are gathered together into the *Dhammapada*. This collection was completed in the third century BC, probably in Ceylon, in the old classical language of Pāli. Its title means 'The Path of the Law', and, although completed many years after Gautama Buddha's death, it is closely linked with him. In its simple statements it sets out the Buddhist ideals of self-mastery and moderation, of righteousness and serenity, of unfailing goodwill and benevolence towards others, and as the ultimate goal the attainment of Nirvāna through the pursuit of truth, detachment and loyalty to the Four Truths taught by the Buddha.

He who drinks of the waters of Truth, he rests in joy with mind serene. The wise find their delight in the Law (the Dhamma), in the Truth revealed by the great.

For he whose mind is well trained in the ways that lead to light, who surrenders the bondage of attachments and finds joy in his freedom from bondage, who free from the darkness of passions shines pure in a radiance of light, even in this mortal life, he enjoys the immortal Nirvāna.

Not to hurt by deeds or words, self-control as taught in the Rules, moderation in food, the solitude of one's room and one's bed, and the practice of the highest consciousness: this is the teaching of the Buddhas who are awake.

Overcome anger by peacefulness; overcome evil by good. Overcome the mean by generosity; and the man who lies by truth.

Speak the truth, yield not to anger, give what you can to him who asks: these three steps lead you to the gods. (15)

These words, recorded two hundred years or so before

Christ and nearly a thousand before Islam was preached by Muhammad are but a few quotations from the *Dhammapada*, of which 'every verse is like a small star and the whole has the radiance of Eternity'. (16):

3. *The Gift of the Torah*

At the beginning and end of the reading of the Torah in the Jewish synagogue service, representatives of the congregation pronounce the blessings which summarize the essentials of the Jewish faith.

Bless the Lord whom we are called to bless.

Blessed be the Lord whom we are called to bless for ever and ever.

Blessed are You, Lord our God, king of the universe, who chose us from all peoples to give us His teaching. Blessed are You Lord, who gives us the Torah.

Blessed are You, Lord our God, king of the universe, who gave us the teaching of truth and planted eternal life within us. Blessed are You, Lord, who gives us the Torah. (17)

These two blessings express the deepest convictions of the Jewish people, that they have been chosen by God to be his people, and that this special relationship is sealed in their acceptance of the Torah as the God-given way by which they are bound always to live.

Torah comes from a root meaning 'to throw, to point, or direct the way', but it is usually translated as 'law', and at its centre are the various laws and regulations given to Moses in the first five books of the Old Testament. Prominent among them are 'the ten commandments', according to tradition written by God on stone tablets and given to Moses.

I am the Lord your God who brought you out of Egypt, when you were slaves.

1. Worship no god but me.
2. Do not make for yourselves images of anything in heaven or on earth or in the water under the earth. Do not bow down to any idol or worship it.
3. Do not use my name for evil purposes.
4. Observe the Sabbath and keep it holy. You have six days in which to do your work, but the seventh day is a day of rest dedicated to me.
5. Respect your father and your mother.
6. Do not commit murder.
7. Do not commit adultery.
8. Do not steal.
9. Do not accuse anyone falsely.
10. Do not desire another man's house ... or anything that he owns. (18)

Other regulations cover the offering of sacrifice, the keeping of feasts, marriage and inheritance, the administration of justice, the rule of the king, the conduct of war, the treatment of slaves, prisoners and foreigners, personal and social hygiene.

Each of the six hundred and thirteen commandments given to Moses is in theory as important as any other, and their large number is held to show that there is no situation in which a commandment could not be fulfilled; they provide every Jewish person with an opportunity of observing the Torah in a specific way. (19) But the Torah is more than the books of the Law, more indeed than all the other scriptures of the Old Testament. The Torah also includes the teaching of the rabbis about the Law, contained mainly in the voluminous writings of the *Talmud* and *Midrash*. In essence Torah means 'all that God has made known of himself, his will and purpose for creation'.

Like Tao and Dharma in other religions, the Jews valued the Torah so highly that they described it in universal terms. ' "The Torah was given in the wilderness and in fire and in water [i.e. to Moses at Sinai in the circumstances described in Exodus 19 and 24]. As these three are free to all the inhabitants of the world, so are the words of the Law free to all the inhabitants of the world." The rabbis seem to suggest that all the nations started on an equal footing; what distinguishes Israel is their glad acceptance of the great treasure of Torah.' (20) Not only was the Torah, therefore, universally relevant, but it was also believed to have been created before the world itself; 'the Law because it is more highly prized than everything was created before everything, as it is said, "The Lord created me as the beginning of his way".' Thus 'the world was created for the sake [literally: because of the merit] of the Torah'. In the words of Simon the Just, recorded in the *Pirkey Avot*, a collection of sayings first compiled a hundred years after Jesus, 'The world stands upon three things: the Torah, worship and the showing of kindness.' (21)

The Torah, in this developed sense, became identified with Wisdom, the beneficent ordering of existence, active in nature and in human society because of God's sovereign rule in creation and in history. The identification of Wisdom with the Torah was first made in the book of

Ecclesiasticus (24, 23); thereafter it became commonplace, and had great influence in suggesting that the Torah is of universal significance not only for men, but for the whole creation. (22)

Thus the Torah was closely associated with God: 'If two sit together and words of Torah are between them, the *Shechinah* [i.e. the glory of the divine presence] rests between them.' Moreover, 'this enabled the rabbis to say that when God gave the Torah to Israel he was giving himself, since he cannot be altogether separated from his Torah.' (23) But in contrast with the Muslim attitude towards the Qur'ān, the Torah is never dissociated from the created universe. Although it has, in some respects, a heavenly as well as an earthly existence, it is created by God and the expression, not the essence, of his mind and will. Indeed the respect which the Jewish rabbis gave to the Torah must be set alongside their constant recognition of the presence of God, the sovereign being on whose will alone the whole universe depends. At the heart of the Jewish faith is their belief that the living God, the sovereign king of the universe who confronts them in all the events of their history, gave them the Torah as the Way of life according to his will which they are to follow.

The living God O magnify and bless,
Transcending Time and here eternally.

One Being, yet unique in unity;
mystery of Oneness measureless.

Lo! form or body he has none, and man
No semblance of his holiness can frame.

Before Creation's dawn he was the same;
The first to be, though never he began.

He is the world's and every creature's Lord;
His rule and majesty are manifest,

And through his chosen, glorious sons exprest
In prophecies that through their lips are poured.

Yet never like to Moses rose a seer,
Permitted glimpse behind the veil divine.

This faithful prince of God's prophetic line
Received the Law of Truth for Israel's ear.

The Law God gave he never will amend,
Nor ever by another Law replace. (24)

To keep that Law has been the privilege and pride of the
Jewish people down through the centuries. Its commandments and their implications have touched every facet of
their lives, secular and civic as well as religious and
personal, and in keeping them with scrupulous care Jews
have often appeared to be alien to the communities in
which they have lived. Their distinctive dress and their
rule of life, laid down in the Torah, have often made them
uncomfortable neighbours. The pressure indeed has been
so great as to cause division within the Jewish community
itself, between the Orthodox who keep every detail of the
Torah with scrupulous care, and the Liberal Jews who
emphasize the spirit rather than the details of the Torah.
But its teaching has enriched the whole Jewish community,
and has been their constant inspiration. By this they have
lived and by this they have triumphed over persecution
and adversity. The Torah has played a decisive role in
preserving the identity and integrity of the Jewish people.
Above all it has given them the courage and the confidence to believe that wherever the Torah has been kept

there the kingly rule of God has been with them for blessing.

Potentially that blessing is for all mankind, as a prayer for the Sabbath Evening Service in a modern Jewish Prayer Book makes clear.

It is our duty to praise the Lord of all, to recognize the greatness of the creator of first things, who has chosen us from all peoples by giving us His Torah. Therefore we bend low and submit, and give thanks before the King above the kings of kings, the Holy One, blessed be He ...

Therefore, Lord our God, we put our hope in You. Soon let us witness the glory of Your power; when the worship of material things shall pass away from the earth, and prejudice and superstition shall at last be cut off; when the world will be set right by the rule of God, and all mankind shall speak out in Your name, and all the wicked of the earth shall turn to You. Then all who inhabit this world shall meet in understanding, and shall know that to You alone each one shall submit, and pledge himself in every tongue. In Your presence, Lord our God, they shall bow down and be humble, honouring the glory of Your being. All shall accept the duty of building Your kingdom, so that Your reign of goodness shall come soon and last forever. For Yours alone is the true kingdom, and only the glory of Your rule endures forever. So it is written in Your Torah:

'The Lord shall rule for ever and ever.'

So it is prophesied:

'The Lord shall be as a king over all the earth
On that day the Lord shall be One, and known as One.' (25)

The will and grace of God, revealed in the Torah, are in Jewish eyes the Way of life; on this basis well-being, prosperity and salvation may be enjoyed by all mankind.

4. *The Road to the Well*

Muslim religious law is based upon two sources: the Qur'ān, the Word of God, and the Traditions. These latter record what those who had been the companions of Muhammad had to tell about his actions and words in answer to the requests of the Muslim community for guidance. They mostly describe: how the Prophet had behaved in particular circumstances: what decisions he had made in disputes and legal matters referred to him: what his manners, dress and habits had been: what he had allowed, or forbidden, to be done in his presence: and any striking saying which he had uttered, or significant action which he had performed.

During the early years of the Arab empires many spurious Traditions were invented to serve particular interests, political, social or doctrinal, but in time more careful study and evaluation of the Traditions resulted in greater discrimination being exercised in regard to them. The Traditions kept alive for the Muslim community the memory of the Prophet's life and sayings as the Qur'ān itself could never have done. In some respects they are similar to the Christian Gospels, but in a way which is at the same time both more detailed and also more open to corruption. Attitudes towards them varied considerably during the first two centuries, but, by the time of the great lawyer al-Shāfiʿī (died AD 820), the overriding authority of the *sunna*, or customary practice, of Muhammad, as established by the Traditions, was generally accepted. The sunna has in fact given its name to the majority of Muslims who are known as *Sunnis* in contrast to the minority of *Shī'ite* Muslims.

All Muslims are called to follow the one path of conduct laid down in the Qur'ān, and the *sunna* of the Prophet. It is called the *Sharī'a*, a word originally meaning 'the road to the watering place' which, in the circumstances of Arabia, was clearly marked by stones and other signs as well as by the passage of people passing to and fro. With the completion of the Qur'ān's revelation at the death of Muhammad, and after the later work of Muslim jurists and theologians, the Muslim Sharī'a became established. Its two main divisions are the social and political laws and regulations which govern Muslims, and the religious duties which a Muslim owes to God; prayer, fasting in *Ramaḍān*, alms-giving and pilgrimage. (26) In course of time, other codes of law have developed alongside the Sharī'a, particularly in criminal and civil matters, and the relationship between these secular codes of law and the Sharī'a is a matter for dispute in countries where there are large numbers of Muslims, whether in a majority or a minority situation. (27)

The Sharī'a gives great support not only to the individual Muslim but also to the community by providing a framework of reference within which ordinary Muslims feel secure and in sympathy with their neighbours. A fixed but rich and recreative pattern of daily prayer hallows the life of the whole community. The annual month of fasting provides a regular opportunity for self-discipline and restraint. The duty of almsgiving makes people take account of their possessions and remember that they are a trust to be used for the good of others. The institution of pilgrimage reminds every Muslim family of their links with the world-wide community of Islam, irrespective of race or nationality. The duty of *jihād* (literally, 'struggle') which at the beginning was associated with the military needs of the first community in Medina, in its developed form encourages Muslims to give whole-heartedly of themselves and their possessions for the defence and advancement of Islam, and of Muslim states. These are the *'ibādāt*, or obligations of a servant, which a Muslim owes to God, the sovereign lord of the universe. The relationship of servants to their lord which lies behind Muslim religious duties ennobles those who accept it and it is often the vehicle of a profound spirituality. (28)

Other parts of the Sharī'a provide rules to guide Muslims in their personal habits and their social behaviour. Its basis is the personal and communal life of Muhammad and his companions in Mecca and Medina, and an idealized picture of that social pattern inspires much of Muslim apologetics in the contemporary world. Emphasis is placed upon those features of it which some think to be desirable in the present atmosphere of uncertainty about moral standards: the strong sense of community which transcended racial and tribal differences, the protection of seclusion offered to women, the distribution of property among all dependent members of a family upon the death of its householder, compassion shown to the poor, to children and to animals, together with guidance in domestic and personal hygiene. The virtues of forbearance, patience and moderation are praised, not only in personal conduct but in civil law and in economic practice. (29)

The question must be asked, however, whether the Sharī'a, as traditionally understood, can provide the guidance which is needed in the twentieth century. It developed within an environment very different from that in which we now live, and it includes some features which appear in conflict with the contemporary understanding of basic human rights. These include the harsh penalties prescribed for acts of theft and adultery, the prohibition of alcohol, the provision for divorce to be made effective at the husband's will, and the legalization of polygamy. There were incidents in the Prophet's life, particularly in his dealings with the Jewish tribes at Medina, which would not be accepted as models for leaders today. The Sharī'a also gives status to non-Muslim groups which is not in accord with the needs of contemporary pluralist societies.

The Qur'ān and Traditions, however, are not the only foundations on which the Sharī'a is based: associated with them are 'consensus' (*ijmā'*), i.e. of the whole Muslim community, and the use of analogy (*qiyās*) in cases where there is no direct ruling in the two primary sources. Thus a survey, by a Muslim scholar, commented on current trends in the Islamic world: 'The implementation of the Sharī'a need not be an obstance to material progress and mental emancipation ... There is a broad current of Muslim thought – not necessarily all liberal – pointing to the pragmatic spirit of the forebearers who integrated into their system whatever they found useful with others. The core of unalterable prophetic injunctions around which the branches of the law were woven, is not very large, so that there is much scope for adapting the Sharī'a to the changed circumstances.' (30) These principles introduced flexibility into the Sharī'a at an early stage; they create the possibility of further development in the future.

5. *The Road that Leads to Life*

Jesus was born into a society in which the written law of the Old Testament had already become accepted as authoritative and in which the Jewish rabbis were beginning to develop the oral commentary, the *Halacha*, which two centuries later was incorporated in the *Mishnah* and then the *Talmud*. Thus he lived in a society which was dominated by acceptance of the Torah and obedience to the provisions of the Law on the part of religious people, particularly the lawyers and the Pharisees. Jesus accepted the role of a rabbi, gave much of his teaching in rabbinic form and disputed with rabbis upon points arising out of the interpretation of the Torah. But he also criticized the way in which his contemporaries handled the Torah, and taught a different 'road to life' for his disciples to follow. (31)

Jesus knew, used and loved the Old Testament scriptures, but his attitude towards them was determined by his living awareness of God's unconditional grace and his belief that God's kingdom had already dawned. Indeed he made friends of those groups in society which, for various reasons, were unable to keep the regulations of the law as the rabbis interpreted it; the artisans and peasants who could not follow the precise and costly regulations for ritual purification, and tax-collectors who worked with non-Jews, were the very ones whom Jesus invited to share in God's kingdom. His mission was directed, in intention at least, not only to the Jews who kept the Law, but to all other human beings as well. His ministry in Galilee reached beyond the boundaries of the Jewish settlements, and, in his attempt to purify the Temple worship, he tried to make its Court of the Gentiles a 'house of prayer for all the nations'. In his teaching he did not hesitate to criticize the written Law itself; for example, he sharpened its prohibitions against murder and adultery to include anger and lust, and he rejected its provisions for divorce; his declaration of the obligation to love without discrimination overturned the provisions of the Law for just retaliation, and for precise definitions of the obligations of neighbourliness. (32)

As far as the oral law of the rabbis was concerned, Jesus rejected much of it as 'the commandments of men'; rules about the sabbath depreciated human dignity – 'the Sabbath was made for the sake of man and not man for the Sabbath' – and rules about purification not only ignored the real source of evil in personal attitudes but also deprived men of enjoying the blessedness of God's kingdom. (33) Jesus made these criticisms of the law, both as expressed in the scriptures and by contemporary rabbis, not capriciously but because of his belief in the generous grace of God. The Old Testament 'You shall be holy, because I, the Lord your God, am holy' was replaced by emphasis on the love and goodness of God, the heavenly Father. 'There must be no limit to your goodness, as your heavenly Father's goodness knows no bounds.' In making this call Jesus was not destroying the Law but bringing it to completion; his disciples would only enter God's kingdom if they showed themselves better men than the Pharisees and the doctors of the Law. (34) We should realize, however, that Jesus' criticisms were directed specifically towards the teaching of his contemporaries and not towards the teaching of Judaism as it has developed during later centuries.

The criticism which Jesus made of contemporary Jewish teaching was, however, secondary to the description of 'the road to life' which he gave to his disciples. 'The road that leads to perdition is wide with plenty of room,' he said, 'and many go that way; but the road that leads to life is small and narrow, and those who find it are few.' In helping them to find it, he invited people, both men and women, to share in his mission. Like him they were to be 'fishers of men' and he would send them out as the messengers of God's kingdom. He invited them to be his disciples. (35)

As we shall see in greater detail in the next chapter, Jesus taught his disciples to live in the reality of God's kingdom; he helped them to enter into its blessings and its joys, and he taught them a style of life appropriate to it. He set out this style of life most clearly in a poem, often called 'the Beatitudes', which appears to have been polished by repetition on many occasions. Matthew's Gospel placed it at the beginning of the great sermon preached by Jesus on a hill in Galilee and in so doing emphasized the contrast between the teaching of Jesus and the Law which, according to tradition, had been given to the Jews on Mount Sinai.

'When Jesus saw the crowds he went up the hill. There he took his seat, and when his disciples had gathered round him he began to address them. And this is the teaching he gave:

'How blest are those who know their need of God;
   the kingdom of Heaven is theirs.
How blest are the sorrowful;
   they shall find consolation.
How blest are those of a gentle spirit; they shall have
   the earth for their possession.
How blest are those who hunger and thirst to see right
   prevail; they shall be satisfied.

How blest are those who show mercy; mercy shall be
shown to them.
How blest are those whose hearts are pure; they shall see
God.
How blest are the peacemakers; God shall call them his
sons.
How blest are those who have suffered persecution for the
cause of right; the kingdom of Heaven is theirs.' (36)

In the first of these eight stanzas Jesus made it clear that
'the good life' depends upon a relationship of worship and
of trust towards God; the resources of his kingdom are
available to those who know their need of him. In the
other stanzas Jesus emphasized the commitment to God's
kingdom which is asked of those who know the blessedness
of being members of it. This commitment may cause them
to suffer hunger and thirst in seeking for its coming, to
endure persecution in its service and to engage actively
in the making of peace. Above all their style of living is
to be marked by a gentleness and compassion towards
others which show them to be God's children. In teaching
that to love one's neighbour is the greatest commandment
after loving God, Jesus put in a positive form the teaching
of the Rabbi Hillel (c. 20 BC) that 'not to do to another
what seems to you to be hurtful' was the whole Torah,
on which all the rest is commentary. (37) But he did more
than this; he extended neighbourliness to include the poor,
the needy, and even one's enemies. To be his disciple
meant a life of love which could only be sustained by a
daily denial of self-interest and ambition: 'none of you
can be a disciple of mine,' he said, 'without parting with
all his possessions.' Only so could people act with the
generosity to the needy for which Jesus asked. (38)

People cannot, however, accept this teaching, much less act upon it, without a radical transformation of the inner focus of their lives. Hence the emphasis which Jesus placed upon the need for repentance: 'The time has come,' he said, 'the kingdom of God is upon you; repent, and believe the Gospel.' The call for repentance was an essential element in his preaching, to be set alongside his declaration that 'whoever does not accept the kingdom of God like a child will never enter it', and his call for self-forgetfulness. He reproached the cities where he ministered because they gave no sign of repentance and when he sent out the twelve apostles on a mission, the Gospel writer says, 'they set out and called publicly for repentance'. Jesus taught that repentance was not just regret for the past, nor even a new attempt to do better than before and to try harder. As radical as 'the new birth' which he asked of Nicodemus, repentance meant 'a return of the whole personality to God, a submission of the will to his will, the acceptance of his sovereignty. It is by this act of submission that the kingdom of God is entered, and it is this decisive change that is presupposed in the detailed teaching of Jesus. The change itself is made possible by the new experience of God as Jesus reveals him, that is, as the merciful and loving Father who seeks and saves the lost.' The life of joy and blessing, spoken of in the Beatitudes, is possible to achieve, because when man identifies his will with the will of God he makes his life 'part and parcel of the purpose of God in the world'. Repentance brings joy, as when a lost sheep is found or a son given up for good makes his way home; it is the prelude to the joyous banquet of God's kingdom, the wedding garment which a man must put on to share in it. (39)

The style of life which Jesus invited his disciples to learn and to adopt was that by which he lived himself. He lived a life of self-giving, going out into the villages to teach and to heal because he was moved with compassion towards those who needed a physician, a shepherd to care for them. 'Jesus went round visiting all the towns and villages. He taught in the synagogues, preached the Good News about the Kingdom, and healed people with every kind of disease and sickness. As he saw the crowds, his heart was filled with pity for them, because they were worried and helpless, like sheep without a shepherd.' Living himself in dependence upon God and spending long hours in prayer, he used the resources of God's kingdom to bring healing to others. He was gentle and compassionate towards the possessed and the outcasts. He sought to bring peace, among his own disciples and in the lives of men – avaricious Zacchaeus, impetuous Peter – and he knew himself the bitterness of persecution and hostility. He said 'no' to himself and carried his own cross to Golgotha. (40)

His teaching was of a way of life and not a set of rules; it was a style which all could learn and which was expressed in many different ways. The teaching of Jesus has become the inspiration for successive generations of Christians down through the ages; it continues, in our own times, to be realized in life-styles which are authentically Christian but expressed, as they must be if they are to be real, in contemporary idioms and directed towards specific issues.

During the period immediately after the passion and resurrection of Jesus, his apostles concentrated on proclaiming the good news of the resurrection and declaring the mission of Jesus as the Messiah. Those who became

Christians in response to their preaching, however, soon demanded guidance about what it meant to live as Christians, and in meeting this need the apostles used what they remembered of the teaching of Jesus, as well as the conventional moral teaching of their times. The Gospels show how authoritative his message was for the first Christian churches, and, although there are few direct quotations of Jesus' words in the Epistles, they contain very many indirect echoes of his teaching. The main themes in the fifth chapter of Peter's first letter, for example, shepherding, humility, watchfulness, God's care, brotherhood, peace, echo very closely the words of Christ himself. (41) The dependence of the first Christians on the teaching and example of Jesus is clearly demonstrated in the letters of St Paul. 'When Paul had to impress certain ethical duties upon his converts he appealed to what Jesus essentially was and did. In writing to the Philippians to inculcate humility he urges: "Let this mind be in you, which was also in Christ Jesus ... who humbled Himself, and became obedient unto death, even the death of the Cross". Similarly, liberality is commended to the Corinthians through a reminder of Him "who though He was rich, yet for our sakes became poor". It has often been plausibly suggested that the exhortation to, and description of, *love* in 1 Corinthians is based upon the life of Jesus, is in short a kind of character sketch of the Lord ... In a real sense conformity to Christ, His teaching and His life, has taken the place for Paul of conformity to the Jewish Torah. Jesus Himself – in word and deed – in fact is a New Torah.' (42)

One of the most important of the words of Jesus is his invitation 'Come to me, all whose work is hard, whose load is heavy; and I will give you relief. Bend your necks to my yoke, and learn from me for I am gentle and humble-hearted; and your souls will find relief. For my yoke is good to bear, my load is light.' In these words, Jesus made a deliberate contrast with the yoke of the Torah which the Jewish believer took upon himself. Thus, for example, the Rabbi Nechunya (c. AD 70) said: 'He that takes upon himself the yoke of the Law, from him shall be taken away the yoke of the kingdom [i.e. the oppression of worldly powers] and the yoke of worldly care.' But Jesus declared the rabbis' teaching to be oppressive; in contrast with theirs the style of life to which he called his disciples was easy to bear, joyful and sustaining, because it was linked with the kingdom of God and his grace. Ben Sirach, the author of *Ecclesiasticus*, claimed that by submitting to the yoke of the Torah he had found great peace: Jesus promised peace to those who learnt from him the way of love for God and for man. (43)

Postscript

We have discussed, in this chapter, the patterns of conduct which are associated with the most wide-spread of the world's 'religions', excluding Hinduism and Marxism: these are, to use Tolstoy's phrase, 'what men live by'.

Each particular way has its own characteristics and its own basic dynamic:

the calm dignity of the Chinese philosophies, which teach how to live in harmony with the fundamental pattern of things as they are: the quest of Buddhists for self-mastery and self-negation and for a positive and loving attitude towards others: the faithfulness of the Jewish people to the Torah which reveals the will of God and holds the secret of well-being for themselves and the whole creation: the loyal service which Muslims offer to God, whose servants they are, in the regular practice of prayer, fasting and alms-giving, and in faithfulness to the pattern given to the community in the days of Muhammad, their apostle: the way of love to which Christians aspire as disciples of Jesus, in response to God's fatherly grace and as citizens of his coming kingdom.

There are profound and important differences between these ways of life, not only in detail, but above all in the nature of the relationship which they teach exists between the Creator and his creatures, and in the word through which they believe he has revealed his will to men. They have also, however, much in common, for they all affirm that human people are capable of living good, generous and moral lives and that they are under obligation to live according to those ideals. They define the obligation in different ways, but always for the good of the community as a whole, with mastery of the self as its necessary counterpart. They agree in condemning acts of aggression against others by word or deed, and in commending gentleness, generosity, sincerity of intention and humility.

The life-styles set out here, are, of course, abstractions; their substance is the endless variety of human stories in which the nature of any community is expressed, shaped, enhanced or depreciated by its individual members. The life which each person lives is unique, but its substance is common to us all. In that simple fact lies the possibility of community between individuals, and the hope of working towards a more universal society.

NOTES

1. For references see chapter 2, n. 20.
2. See e.g. *Analects*, IX, 5.
3. See V. Che-chen-tao in *Religions*, 206–9.
4. Op. cit., 208.
5. Lau, op. cit., 32.
6. *Tao-Te-Ching*, chapter 7 (W).
7. Op. cit., chapter 30 (W).
8. Op. cit., chapter 9 (W).
9. Op. cit., chapter 57 (L).
10. Op. cit., chapter 23. This translation is that by J. Shih in *Religions*, 290.
11. See chapter 2, section 2 and chapter 5.
12. See chapter 2, pages 59–60.
13. de Silva, in *A Guide to Religions*, 128–9, and Lamotte, *Towards the Meeting with Buddhism*, Vol. I, 27–30.
14. Christmas Humphreys, *The Buddhist Way of Life*, London, 1969, 76–81.
15. *The Dhammapada*, translated by Juan Mascaro, Penguin Books, 1973, 79, 89, 185, 223, 224.
16. Mascaro, op. cit., 33.
17. See W. W. Simpson, *Jewish Prayer and Worship*, London, SCM, 1965, 40. The translation is from *Forms of Prayer for Jewish Worship*, OUP, 1977, 157 and 159.
18. Exodus 20. 1–17.
19. See P. Schneider, *Sweeter than Honey*, SCM, 1966, 149–153.
20. Cf. Schneider, op. cit., 143.
21. W. D. Davies, *Paul and Rabbinic Judaism*, SPCK, 1947, 170–1.
22. Davies, op. cit., 168–9: von Rad, op. cit., 165–6.

23. *Pirkey Avot* 3. 3: Schneider, op. cit., 148.
24. From the *Yigdal*, composed in Rome about 1300 AD, and sung at the beginning of all synagogue services. W. W. Simpson, *Jewish Prayer and Worship*, 105–6.
25. *Forms of Prayer for Jewish Worship*, 41–3.
26. e.g. N. J. Coulson, *A History of Islamic Law*, Edinburgh, 1964: *A Guide to Religions*, 210–16.
27. See J. Schacht, 'Sharī'a', in *Shorter Encyclopaedia of Islam*.
28. See C. Padwick, *Muslim Devotions*, SPCK, 1961.
29. See Charis Waddy, *The Muslim Mind*, Longmans, 1976: Khurshid Aḥmad (Editor), *Islam, its Meaning and Message*, Islamic Council of Europe, London, 1976, 37.
30. D. H. Khalid, 'The Phenomenon of Re-Islamization', *Aussen Politik*, Hamburg, vol. 29, No. 4, 433–53.
31. Davies, op. cit., 143. See also T. W. Manson, *The Sayings of Jesus*, SCM, 1949, 11–12.
32. See Matthew 9. 10–17: 4. 12–25: Mark 11. 15–19: compare Exodus 20, 13–14 with Matthew 5. 21–2 and 27–8: Deuteronomy 24. 1 with Mark 10. 1–9: Leviticus 24. 19–20 with Matthew 5. 38–48.
33. Mark 2. 18–28 and Matthew 15. 1–20.
34. Leviticus 19. 2 (NEB): Matthew 5. 48 (NEB): 5. 17–20. For a discussion of Jesus' attitude to the Torah see J. Jeremias, *New Testament Theology*, Volume 1, SCM, 1971, 204–211.
35. Matthew 7. 13–14 (NEB margin): 10. 1–8: Mark 1. 16–20. 2. 13–14: 3. 13–19.
36. Matthew 5. 1–10 (NEB).
37. See Jeremias, op. cit., 212.
38. Mark 12. 28–34: Matthew 7. 12: Matthew 25. 31–46: Luke 14. 12–14, 25–33.

39. T. W. Manson, op. cit., 35–7: Mark 1. 15: 10. 13–15: 6. 12 (NEB): Luke 15: Matthew 22. 11–14.

40. Matthew 9. 35–7: Mark 1. 35–9: Luke 6. 12: 8. 1–3: Mark 1. 40–45: 5: Luke 7. 11–17; 36–50: 19: 1–10.

41. See E. G. Selwyn, *The First Epistle of St Peter*, Macmillan, 1949, 23–4: Davies, op. cit., 122–30 and 136–145.

42. Davies, op. cit., 147–8.

43. Matthew 11. 28–30 (NEB): The passage is discussed in detail in T. W. Manson, op. cit., 185–7: Ecclesiasticus 51. 23–7.

CHAPTER 5

Communion

1. *The Path to Communion*

At the heart of religious experience and practice is response to the transcendent; this response takes many forms. Hinduism, in its more philosophical aspects, seeks for realization of the unity between the individual human soul and Brahman. Buddhists have as their ideal the practice of the Dharma taught by the Buddha, but, in popular forms of Buddhism, prayers and offerings are directed towards symbols of the Buddha, his relics and his statues. The prayer-act also plays an important and central part in the practice of Islam.

In this section I wish to consider the more personal and interior aspects of prayer, contemplation and meditation, which recur in similar ways in the experience of Christians, Muslims and others, including Zen Buddhists. This latter group has been prominent first in China and then in Japan since about the fifth century AD, and its members seek to attain enlightenment through particular techniques of contemplative meditation. (1) The pattern which I outline here must also be set in relationship with the techniques of yoga (see page 40), and the bhakti practices of Hinduism which we discuss later in this chapter.

The initial stage of meditative prayer is normally *the prayer of attention*, in which the worshippers attend to the divine presence, and prepare themselves to respond.

In Islam, this stage is represented by the *niyya*, 'the intention', which must preface every act of worship. This need be no more than the expressed intention uttered by the worshipper before prayer; he might say the following words: 'I stand facing the *qibla* [i.e. in the direction of Mecca, marked out in every mosque], and, raising my hands to the level of my ears, I say: "I make my intention to perform the two prostrations of the prescribed prayer-rite of the morning hour."' The niyya is also, however, a spiritual discipline: the prayer to which it is the prelude, is to be recited 'with a whole heart and a sincere intention and entire concentration of one's powers'. (2) Outside the context of prayer, the practice of 'making the right intention' is universal among Muslims; no pious Muslim will begin a task or write a letter without making the invocatory declaration, 'In the name of God, the Compassionate and the Merciful.' In other religions also there are specific ways in which the worshipper recollects himself in the presence of God, and directs his attention towards him. By use of the sacred word and the sacred symbol, the worshipper fixes his attention on God: in Christian usage a phrase of scripture, invocation of the Trinity, the sign of the cross, or reverence towards the sanctuary and its symbols or towards an ikon. (3) Every act of Buddhist worship begins with the recital of the formula of homage to the Buddha – 'Homage to Him, the Blessed One, the Exalted One, the fully Enlightened One.'

The prayer of attention may be followed by *the prayer of quiet*, in which the human person becomes aware of the divine presence which overwhelms him with peace and stillness. 'Essentially, devotion is to be able to sit still and do nothing and receive the divine presence. This is very difficult, there are all kinds of distraction, and many things that pull us away from developing this ability. The essence is stillness.' (4) This Muslim statement is close in intention, though very different in the method of attaining it, to the practices of yoga. 'The spiritual tradition of the East, and especially of India, has been so strongly drawn towards the prayer of silence that it has continually striven to find methods, either physiological or psychological, which can help man to enter upon and travel safely on the way of silence ... As traditionally understood, yoga, is a discipline whose essential aim is to bring the mind to complete quiet and silence.' (5)

The prayer of quiet merges into *the prayer of communion* and is often undistinguished from it. Thoughts and emotions are stilled, and the whole personality is for the moment integrated in a living rapport with the object of worship. The one who prays is enabled to be totally occupied with the divine object. 'The aim of prayer, indeed, is not to think about God, not to form conceptions of God, however strong and lofty they may be. It is for God himself, for God beyond any sign or any veil, that the soul, fed by the Gospel and the Spirit, is thirsty. It is God in himself whom the soul wants, the living God revealed to the patriarchs and the prophets, the hidden God within, the God who is realized in the contemplation of saints and sages.' (6)

'The saints of God are known by three signs,' said the Muslim Ṣūfī, Dā'ūd ibn Nusair (d. AD 872): 'Their thought is of God, their dwelling is with God, their business is with God.' His words are illustrated in the writings of the Muslim Rābi'a of Baṣra who lived towards the end of the eighth century AD. It is said that at night she used to go up onto her roof and pray thus: 'O my Lord, the stars are shining and the eyes of men are closed, and kings have shut their doors and every lover is alone with his beloved, and here I am alone with Thee.'

Two ways I love Thee: selfishly,
And next, as worthy is of Thee.
'Tis selfish love that I do naught
Save think on Thee with every thought.
'Tis purest love when Thou dost raise
The veil to my adoring gaze.
Not mine the praise in that or this:
Thine is the praise in both, I wis. (7)

The final stage on the road of contemplation is *the prayer of the kingdom*. Caught up into communion with God the worshipper goes out into the world which is God's creation to seek his kingdom and his glory. As St John of the Cross put it, at the beginning one sees the creator through his creatures, but at the end one sees the creatures through the creator. This stage in Zen teaching is called 'the return to the market-place' and it is the fruit of all creative prayer. (8) 'Real prayer does not mean running away from life; quite the contrary. It produced in Thomas Merton, contemplative as he was, a concern for social justice. "Contemplation is the spring," he wrote, "action the stream."' (9) At the conclusion of the prayer-rite, the Muslim solemnly gives the greeting of peace; in thankfulness to God for his peace, and in greeting to the Prophet, the angels and his fellow-believers. He is ready again for involvement in the world. (10)

The four stages outlined above are not fixed stages through which a person passes consecutively within a sequence of time; they describe, rather, different aspects of contemplative prayer, which occur either consecutively or concurrently, and all of which have to be rediscovered and renewed time and again. Many other descriptions are possible, and the Ṣūfīs of Islam traditionally identified a dozen stages or steps in the soul's journey to God. 'Beginning with repentance and abnegation, the soul passed through the long road of dispossession to absorption into God. First the disciple was "one who desired", a *murīd*, then a wayfarer of the spirit, a *sālik*, and finally a sharer of the secret, a *waṣīl*, an initiate.' (11)

A modern statement of the road to communion with God which draws together many strands already studied in this book with reference to Islam, is the advice given by a modern Ṣūfī teacher in Iran, Sheikh M. Hassan Saleh Alishah. He describes the steps which a man must take to draw near to God as follows.

1. SHARI'AT or 'the Law' is the outward discipline of complete obedience to ethical and ritual requirements, in behaviour and worship; Shari'at is a discipline open to every man and woman, from the simplest to the most erudite.

2. ṬARIQAT or 'the Way' is the inner discipline of total obedience to the call of the Spirit in the heart, calling for the abandonment of every high thing that exalts itself against the knowledge of God, the total subordination of the self, the elimination of self-will, the renunciation of every secondary interest and predilection, the dethroning of every idol and enthroning of the one passion to know God and do His Will alone; Ṭariqat is a discipline open to all who have succeeded in bringing their own lives into conformity with *Shari'at*.

3. ḤAQIQAT or 'the Truth' is the entry into the Spirit-filled service of God which is perfect freedom, by which the soul comes to know God and enjoy him for ever ...

Haqiqat is given on earth only to such rare souls as make steps (1) and (2) the only way of life they know or want to live. (12)

Quite often the practice of ceaseless, constant prayer is sustained by the repetition of a particular short prayer or of a divine name. Orthodox Christians are taught to use the Jesus Prayer and to repeat it as often as possible throughout the day. 'Whether you are standing or sitting, walking or lying down, continually repeat "Lord Jesus Christ, have mercy on me." Say it quickly and without hurry, but without fail exactly three thousand times a day without deliberately increasing or diminishing the number. God will help you and by this means you will reach also the unceasing activity of the heart.' (13) Many Muslims repeat the names of God at moments of quiet throughout the day, telling their rosaries as they do so. The *Ṣūfīs*, however, lay particular emphasis upon repetition of the divine name *Allāhu*, either by itself or in the formulas *Allāhu 'Akbar*, 'God is most great', or in the credal statement *Lā 'ilāha 'illa llāh*, 'there is no god except *Allāh*.' Repetition of these phrases can induce trance or ecstasy, or when practised communally can be accompanied by music or dancing. (14)

Hindus also use the names of their deities to enable them to grasp a vision of God. 'They called God "*Shiva*", the Benevolent One, the Auspicious One; "*Rāma*", the Lovely One. They charged those syllables with all the spiritual power of their love and of their adoration. Others after them continued repeating those names and they also enriched them with their own faith and inner experience. Disciples received them from their *gurus* in the sacred rites of initiation. Successive generations of men were called to draw out spiritual energy from them and to make them in return more and more expressive of the highest Mystery. The name indeed is believed to contain in itself as in a nutshell the whole divine Mystery … By the very power it enfolds within itself, invocation of the Name leads the soul towards the very centre, the origin, the unique Source. It endows her with a spiritual energy which will never stop short of divine union.' (15)

2. *The Lord's Song*

The Bhagavad-Gītā, *The Lord's Song*, has a unique and glorious place within the vast range of Hindu Sanskrit literature. It was written somewhere between 500 and 150 BC, and is now part of the *Mahābhārata*, a great epic poem which describes the war between the Kauravas and the Pāndavas for the sovereignty of Hastinapura in northern India. (16) The Mahābhārata describes the struggle between these two families in over a hundred thousand verses, but the *Gītā* is linked to one particular episode only. Arjuna, one of the Pāndava brothers, is persuaded by the driver of his chariot to do his duty and to fight; but the charioteer is the divine *Krishna* who represents in personal form Brahman, the universal source of all that exists. The poem begins with Arjuna's expression of despair:

O Krishna, when I see these kinsmen present here in act to fight,
My limbs grow faint, my mouth is parched, trembling lays hold upon my body, and my hair stands erect; …
Adverse omens I behold, Krishna, nor if I kill my kinsmen in the fight do I foresee any good.
I desire not victory, Krishna, nor yet sovereignty, nor

pleasure. What have we to do with sovereignty? What with delights or life? ...

Thus spoke Arjuna on the field of battle, and sat down upon the chariot seat, dropping his arrows and his bow, his soul o'erwhelmed with grief. The Blessed Lord (Krishna) said:

Never can the embodied soul – [i.e. the real self] – be slain in the body of any; therefore for no being shouldst thou grieve.
Again, if thou considerest thy duty, thou shouldst not waver; for nothing is better for a warrior than a fight decreed by duty.
Happy the warriors, who find a fight like this, that comes without their seeking! It is heaven's gate thrown wide!
But if thou wilt not wage this war, as duty bids, then wilt thou cast aside thy duty and thine honour, and incur guilt.
Slain, thou shalt win heaven; victorious, thou shalt enjoy the earth; therefore arise, with no uncertain spirit for the fight! (17)

The dialogue between Arjuna and Krishna, which is the substance of the poem, begins with a discussion of duty as a way by which man comes to a knowledge of God; the appropriate duty of the warrior class, the *kshatriyas*, is to fight whether in a just or an unjust war, and 'to do one's duty is to worship God'. But Krishna is an incarnation in human form of Brahman, and the poem goes on to discuss every aspect of the relationship between God and man. We have already discussed, in chapter 2, the teachings of philosophical Hinduism about the relationship between *ātman*, the essential self, and Brahman, the universal source of all that is. The Gītā uses many of the terms of the Upanishads but it expounds this relationship in a much more personal way. Short as the Gītā is, it contains many passages of great beauty and insight and it has been an inspiration to millions of Hindus through the centuries. A few passages central to the poem cluster round the great vision of the divine glory which occurs in the eleventh chapter. These extracts will give some idea of the major themes which are the Gītā's continuing contribution to Hinduism and to the human quest for God: the universal, all-pervading glory and sovereignty of Brahman; the qualities in Brahman which call for a personal response from the worshipper; the need for the divine glory to be translated into a human form more intelligible to human worshippers; the primacy of divine grace.

The first extract comes from the passage in which Krishna declared the universal presence of Brahman in the universe in response to Arjuna's prayer that he might come to know him as he is.

Krishna:
'I am the origin of all; all issues forth from me; believing this, the wise devoutly worship me, filled full with love. Their thought on me, their life absorbed in me, teaching one another and speaking ever of me, they are delighted and content. To those men, ceaselessly controlled [i.e. by the discipline of yoga], who worship with affectionate devotion, I give that union with discernment whereby they come to me.

Abiding in their souls, for pity's sake I destroy with the brilliant lamp of knowledge their darkness born of ignorance.'

Arjuna:

'Brahman Supreme, Supreme Abode, thou art Supreme in purifying power! Person eternal and divine, the primal Lord of Heaven, unborn pervading all ...

Thyself alone dost know thy Self by Self, O person Supreme,

O Source of beings, Lord of beings, Lord of Heaven's Lords,

O Ruler of the universe! ...

How may I know thee, in constant meditation? And in what various aspects should I think of thee, O blessed Lord?

Tell me again in full thy work and thy pervading power; for I am never tired of hearing thy words of life.'

Krishna:

'Lo, I will tell thee my pervading powers divine – those that are chief, for there is no limit to my greatness.

I am the Self, Arjuna, dwelling in the heart of every being;

I am the Beginning and Middle of beings, and their End likewise.

Of Sun-Spirits I am *Vishnu*; of lights, the radiant Sun; of Storm-Spirits I am *Mārici* [chief of the *Maruts*, lords of wind and sun]; of the lights of night, the Moon.

Of Vedas I am the *Sāma-veda*; of Heaven's Lords, *Indra* [chief of the gods, see page 68]; of senses I am the Mind; of beings, Consciousness.

(There follows a list of other great beings, natural and supernatural, beneficent and demonic, of which Krishna, personification of Brahman, is 'the Quintessence of all Essences'.)

That also which is the Seed of every being am I, O Arjuna;
nor without me can any being exist that moves or does not move.
Of my pervading powers divine there is no bound, but by examples only have I declared my powers' extent.
Whatever thing has power, prosperity or force, know thou that this is sprung from a part of my glory.
But what avails thee this long lesson, Arjuna? I with one part of myself have established this whole universe, and so abide.' (18)

In response to this declaration of Brahman's universal presence, Arjuna prays that he may be shown God's glory: 'If, Lord, thou thinkest that I am able to look upon it, then reveal to me thy Self immutable.'
In answer, Krishna appears in his divine glory.

If the splendour of a thousand suns were all at once to rise in the sky, that would be like the splendour of that Mighty One.
There in the body of the Lord of Heavenly Lords did Pāndu's son then see the whole universe concentrated, in manifold division.
Then Arjuna, in sore amaze, his hair astir, bowed his head and joining his hands in adoration addressed the Lord of Heaven:
I see, Lord, in thy body all the Lords of Heaven, and divine hosts of beings, Lord *Brahmā* seated on his lotus-throne, and all the seers and snakes divine.

With many arms [i.e. all-powerful], and bellies [i.e. as the storehouse of creatures at their dissolution] and mouths and eyes do I behold thee, on all sides infinite of form; no end in thee, no middle, nor yet beginning do I see, O Universal Lord, O Universal Form!

With crown and mace and disc – a mass of glory gleaming on all sides I behold thee; hardly may I gaze on thee; as burning fire or sun resplendent round about, incomprehensible.

Thou art the Imperishable, learning's highest theme; thou art the supreme treasure-house of this universe; thou art the changeless guardian of eternal law; thou art the Person from everlasting.

With no beginning, middle, or end I see thee; thy might is infinite, thine arms are infinite; the sun and moon thine eyes; thy mouth of kindled fire; with thine own radiance thou dost heat this universe.

For by thee alone are these interspaces of heaven and earth pervaded, and all the quarters of the sky; when it beholds this form of thine, marvellous, terrible, the threefold world shudders, O Mighty One.

Verily unto thee do these hosts of deities draw near; some in affright laud thee with folded hands; crying 'All Hail!', Great Seers and Perfect Ones in hosts praise thee with hymns of praise abounding. (19)

This great vision of the divine glory evoked Arjuna's praise, but as he recalled the fighting in which he was involved he became distressed; Brahman, whose universal glory he had seen in vision, was in fact the Fate which was bringing death to his kinsmen on the field of battle. After another outburst of praise, Arjuna pleaded that he might see Krishna in human form again.

Thou art the Father of this world, of all that moves and does not move; thou art to be adored, its Master reverend; there is none equal unto thee; how could there be a greater in the threefold world, O thou whose power knows no rival?

Therefore I bow myself and prostrate my body and crave grace of thee, the Lord adorable; as father with his son, as comrade with his comrade, as lover with his beloved, so shouldst thou bear with me, O Heavenly Lord!

Now have I seen what none has seen before; therefore am I delighted, though my heart quakes for fear; show me that other form, O Lord of Heaven; be gracious, Lord of Heavenly Lords, Home of the universe!

I wish to see thee even as thou wast [i.e. as his charioteer], with crown, with mace, with disc in hand; take on once more that four-armed shape, O thousand-armed, O Universal Form.

Arjuna's prayer was heard, and Krishna re-appeared, 'assuming pleasant shape' as his charioteer. Seeing again his 'pleasant human form' Arjuna became master of himself and regained his normal state. (20)

This description of Arjuna's vision of God and his response to it emphasizes, in contrast with the teaching of the Upanishads, the personal nature of relationship between man and the transcendent. It emphasizes also devotion or love (*bhakti*) as the way by which the worshipper comes into that living relationship with God which gives salvation. This is not the complete teaching of the Gītā, which also teaches the importance of *jnāna*, inner recollection and discipline of the self, and of *karma*, right action, the duty appropriate to a person's status in life. These also are ways to the knowledge of God which is salvation (21). The supreme importance of devotion, however, is affirmed at the end of Arjuna's vision.

> Krishna said:
> 'Very hard it is to behold that form of mine which thou hast seen; even the Lords of Heaven are ever eager to see that form.
> Neither by the Vedas, nor by austerity, nor by alms, nor yet by sacrifice, can I be seen in such a form as thou hast seen,
> But by devotion undivided, Arjuna, in such a form can I be known, and truly seen, and entered.
> My devotee, whose work is unto me, whose goal I am, free from attachment, void of enmity to any being – he comes to me, Arjuna.' (22)

But human love of God is only a response to the divine love, and, at the end of this great poem, the primacy of divine love is affirmed; salvation consists in responding to that grace with complete self-surrender.

> 'Hear again my highest word, deepest mystery of all; exceeding beloved thou art to me, therefore shall I declare what is thy weal.
> With mind on me devoutly worship me, to me do sacrifice, to me do reverence; to me shalt thou come; true is my promise to thee; thou art dear to me.
> Abandoning every duty, come to me alone for refuge; I will release thee from all sins, sorrow not!' (23)

The commentaries, both Hindu and European, have difficulty in placing this great poem within the development of Hindu thought. It makes use of the classic phraseology, and in places appears to echo the teaching of the Upanishads. (24) But it goes beyond the teaching of the Upanishads in affirming that man is freed, by renunciation and the mastery of himself, to be wholly God's; and that man's highest bliss is participation in the life of God through mutual and personal love between God and himself.

3. *An Intensity of Devotion*

Hinduism embraces many different philosophies and practices, but, in general terms, Hindu teachers have set out three ways in which a human person may come to his ultimate destiny of integration with Brahman, the Infinite and Eternal:

by the performance of religious rituals and sacrifices, and *actions* appropriate to a person's class in society, the way of karma;
by the practice of disciplined meditation and renunciation, the way of *jnāna* (*wisdom*);
by *devotion*, the way of *bhakti*.

Each of these ways was taught in the Gītā, but it culminated in a great vision which affirmed the personal nature of God, and his graciousness, which calls for the response of love from men. (25) This development played a part in the emergence of the bhakti movements within later Hinduism in which intense personal devotion was directed towards one or other of the gods. The concept of a personal God was not entirely new. Since the earliest times of which there is written record, Hindus had worshipped personal deities, the gods and goddesses

of the Vedas, but a new direction had been taken with
the teaching of the Upanishads about Brahman, the one
unchanging Reality behind all existence. Towards the end
of this period further development took place which
recognized the existence of a personal Being, the cosmic
Soul, who is 'other' and 'greater' than the totality of all
things comprehended in Brahman. (26) The *Śvetāśvatara*
Upanishad, for example, spoke in traditional terms about
salvation through the knowledge of Brahman which is
attained through yoga, but it also gave Brahman the
personal names of *Rudra* and *Śiva*, and it concluded by
declaring that he might be known through devotion,
bhakti. A few verses from this Upanishad will illustrate
this development.

Him who is without beginning and without end, in the
midst of confusion,
The Creator of all, of manifold form,
The One embracer of the universe ...
By knowing God one is released from all fetters.

Him who is to be apprehended in existence, who is called
'incorporeal',
The maker of existence and non-existence, the kindly one
(Śiva),
God, the maker of creation and its parts ...
They who know Him, have left the body behind.

When with the nature of the self, as with a lamp,
A practiser of Yoga beholds here the nature of Brahman,
Unborn, steadfast, from every nature free ...
By knowing God one is released from all fetters.

To one who has the highest devotion (bhakti) for God,
And for his spiritual teacher even as for God,
To him these matters become manifest ... (27)

This later development within the Upanishads, as it became linked with the emphasis of the Gītā on a personal relationship with God, made it possible for the bhakti movements to develop in Hinduism alongside the sacrificial rituals of the Vedas. Most humans imagine the transcendent reality whose presence they encounter in the universe, as a person, a *he* (or *she*) not an *it*. The bhakti sects in Hinduism illustrate this quality of religious experience clearly, for the focus in each of them is personal devotion towards one particular god, conceived as the manifestation of Brahman. The meaning of the Sanskrit root from which bhakti comes is 'to share, participate in', and in personal relationships it is used particularly of the loyalty and devotion shown by an inferior to a superior, and of sexual love. (28)

The gods worshipped in the bhakti movements were principally *Śiva*, *Śakti*, his consort, and *Vishnu*. They are mentioned in the Vedas, but not as the principal deities, and their later prominence may be due to a reassertion of earlier native deities against the Aryan deities of the Vedas. Śiva is identified in the *Śvetāśvatara* Upanishad with *Rudra*, the hunter-god of the Rig-Veda, but in the Śiva cults his role is developed in a variety of ways. He represents the vital energy of the universe, symbolized as both male and female, and he is both creator and destroyer, ceaselessly active and yet eternally at rest. He transcends what is simply human, and may appear in any animal form. Despite the fact that he was later to inspire the tenderest love among his devotees, he remains a

mysterium tremendum et fascinosum; 'a mystery which terri-
fies and yet fascinates'. (29)

Vishnu is another of the deities who were of minor
importance in the Vedas but came to prominence in the
bhakti movements. He is portrayed as more gentle than
Śiva and is believed to have become incarnate at different
times in order to rehabilitate the world. His purpose in
doing so is explained by Krishna, one of Vishnu's incarnations, in the Gītā.

> My Self is changeless and unborn and I am Lord of
> every being,
> But using Nature, which is mine, by my own Power
> I come to being.
> For whensoever Righteousness begins to fade away on
> earth,
> Whenever Unrighteousness grows, at once I send myself
> to birth.
> For the protection of the good, for Right to gain
> stability
> And for the wrong to be destroyed, age after age I come
> to be. (30)

Vishnu's incarnations, called in Sanskrit *avatārs*, are
'descents', i.e. the divine being descends to earth in the
guise of a creature for a period in order to assist mankind.
This guise need not be human and Vishnu is said to have
appeared as a fish, a turtle, a boar, a man–lion, and a
dwarf, as well as in human form, including the Buddha;
he is yet to come as *Kalkin*, riding on a white horse, to
purify the world. (31)

Hindu beliefs about the avatārs, especially those in
human form, are sometimes said to be similar to the

Christian doctrine of the incarnation, but they differ in quite fundamental ways. First, the avatārs, or descents, of Vishnu are repeated in various forms, while Christians believe the incarnation of God's Word in Jesus of Nazareth to have been unique and final; it was a complete assumption of humanity and has consequences which affect the whole of creation. Secondly, the avatārs of Vishnu are part of the endless cycle of the ages, the endless alternations of generation and relapse, of activity and rest, which lie behind the universe. By contrast the birth, death and resurrection of Christ are believed to be crucial episodes within the ongoing history of the universe which began at creation and culminates in the Last Judgement and the Eternal City.

The differences between the Hindu and Christian doctrines of incarnation become clear when the four Gospels of the New Testament are contrasted with the much more extended material of Hindu mythology. The Gospels record four accounts of the deeds and words of Jesus of Nazareth as they were told by those who had been his disciples, and retold in the life and witness of the first Christian groups. The stories have been shaped and edited in accordance with the particular interests of the churches, but all through there is direct contact with the actual historical person of Jesus Christ. In marked contrast are the Hindu stories of the gods and the saints, and, particularly, of the incarnations of Vishnu. Even a cursory reading of Hindu stories, or a study of Hindu art, demonstrates how different Hindu mythology is from the testimonies of the Gospels. Its basic theme is the emergence of order out of chaos, and relapse again into chaos, but it is expressed in a bewildering variety of stories. The endless variety of the myth stories is reflected in the complex and bewildering images of the Hindu gods and heroes which appear bizarre to the Western observer who is unfamiliar with the conventions of the underlying mythology. (32)

The avatārs of Vishnu, however, which have had greatest influence in Hinduism were those in human form, his incarnations in Rāma and Krishna. In the earliest version of the story, Rāma was no more than a chivalrous hero, but the myth of Vishnu's avatār was later added in the *Rāmāyana* epic. Rāma was driven from his throne and then robbed of his wife, the beautiful Sītā: she accompanied him to the forest but was captured and taken to Lanka (Ceylon) by the king of the Rākṣasas, Rāvaṇa. Aided by the monkeys, under their hero-king Hanūmat, Rāma waged a long battle with Rāvaṇa, helped also by the Ocean, Nala the smith of the gods, and others. In the end he was victorious and Rāvaṇa was killed in single combat by Rāma's arrows. Sītā was restored to Rāma but later he spurned her as if she had been faithless to him. Sītā in deep grief offered herself on a funeral pyre, but, as the fire was blazing round her, the great gods revealed to Rāma that he was really the god Vishnu who had entered into a mortal man's body in order to slay Rāvaṇa. Sītā was restored to him purified by the fire, 'shining like the young sun, her hair dark and wavy, adorned with gold that had been purified by fire, wearing red garments, and garlands that did not wither', and together they entered heaven. The identification of Rāma with Vishnu is an addition to the original story, but it was developed in later versions in the fourteenth century and by Tulsī Dās in the seventeenth. Rāma remains for contemporary India the perfect model of humanity. Yet, as in the detail of his reunion with Sītā, there are other traits in his character which are unattractive to European readers. (33)

By contrast Krishna, in whom also Vishnu descended to live among men, is a wild, playful youth who delights in making mischief. In the Mahābhārata, Krishna plays a small part only, except in the Gītā where he reveals himself to Arjuna as an incarnation of Brahman. The legend of Krishna in its later developed form in the *Purānas* was built up from many sources, including folk-tales and legends which may originally have had no connection with the god Vishnu. (34) The most important of the stories tell how in infancy he killed the ogress Pūtanā who tried to poison him with milk as she had other infants, how as a boy he overcame the poisonous serpent Kāliya and drove it into the ocean, and as a young man beguiled and played with the goat-girls of his village. Later Krishna married the beautiful Rādhā, having rescued her from marriage to one of his cousins. Mortally wounded by an arrow wound in his heel, Krishna returned radiant to heaven. The story may be understood at many different levels, for although it is a tale of legendary heroism and exotic romantic love, it abounds with mythological themes and may be interpreted in symbolic ways. Underlying it all is the myth of the struggle between good and evil, between life and death. (35)

The strangest of the bhakti deities is Śakti, the consort of Śiva. Symbol of the power by which Śiva creates and destroys, Śakti is worshipped both as a beneficent deity, Umā or Pārvatī, and as a terrifying one, Kālī or Durgā. In this latter aspect she is portrayed as dancing on Śiva's body, festooned with skulls, her tongue lolling out and dripping with blood. Her cult flourished in Bengal in the eighteenth century towards the end of the bhakti period. (36)

The bhakti movement flourished within Hinduism for more than a thousand years, from about AD 600 to 1750. It was carried forward in the vernacular languages, particularly Tamil in the south of India, Hindi, Marathi and Bengali. Although there was no formal break with the rituals and liturgies of the Vedas and the temples, worship in the different bhakti movements was offered through hymns, accompanied by dancing, under the direction of the gurus. The rhythmic singing induced intense emotion and ecstasy which led the worshippers to believe that they were in direct contact with the deities whom they worshipped. Any devotee could join in this worship, and the normal caste regulations were ignored.

At the heart of the bhakti movement was the conviction that a person might attain salvation by being devoted to a personal deity who loves the human soul and seeks for love in return. The soul is completely dependent upon this divine grace, and can do nothing to attain salvation except to commit itself wholly to it.

> Thou gav'st thyself, thou gained'st me;
> Which did the better bargain drive?
> Bliss found I in infinity;
> But what didst thou from me derive?
> O Śiva, Perundurai's God,
> My mind thou tookest for thy shrine;
> My very body's thine abode;
> What can I give thee, Lord, of mine?
>
> I ask not kin, nor name, nor place,
> Nor learned men's society.
> Men's lore for me no value has;
> Kuttālam's lord, I come to thee.

Wilt thou one boon on me bestow,
A heart to melt in longing sweet,
As yearns o'er new-born calf the cow,
In yearning for thy sacred feet?

O madman with the moon-crowned hair
Thou lord of men, thou fount of grace,
How to forget thee could I bear?
My soul hath aye for thee a place.
Venney-nallūr, in 'Grace's shrine'
South of the stream of Pennai, there,
My father, I became all thine;
How could I now myself foreswear? (37)

In the cult of Śiva as it developed among the Tamils there
was a deep sense of man's evil condition and guiltiness
when separated from God, but always the main emphasis
was on the attainment of salvation (*mokṣa*) by abandoning
the self and becoming attached to the saving god, as body
to the soul, as servant to the master, even as beloved to the
lover. This can be seen very clearly in the cult associated
with Krishna. 'The goat-girls' love for the youthful
Krishna became the symbol of the love of the soul for
God, and this self-abandonment to the divine became
central to the cult of Krishna. Every stage in the divine
hero's life, however, was utilized to excite the loving
devotion of his worshippers. As the divine child he
appealed to the maternal instinct, as a youth he became
the lover of the soul, as a young warrior the trusted
companion who is ever at your side, and in his maturity
he became the universal father of all. It was, however,
his love of the goat-girls and their love for him that gave
the cult of Krishna its special flavour; God is in love with

the soul, and the soul with God. In this divine love-affair God is necessarily the male, the soul the female: God takes the initiative and the soul must passively wait for the divine embrace. The Krishna of the *Bhāgavata Purāna* is a very different person from the rather austere Krishna of the Gītā; he is not a teacher, but a lover, the handsome and wayward shepherd-boy who beguiles the soul with the sweet strains of his flute.' (38)

The bhakti movements illustrate the longing of the human soul for deep unifying relationships with the transcendent. They express these longings very powerfully, but, as in other religions, emphasis came to be placed upon emotion and upon the devotion experienced and expressed by the individual worshipper. Moral considerations were never entirely absent, but they were not prominent. The failure of the bhakti movements to deal with social problems diminished their influence in the eighteenth century, when India came into more direct contact with Europe, and efforts were made to assert the traditions of Hinduism or to reform them; but bhakti movements have continued to play their part within Hinduism and a contemporary description of the cult of Krishna in the holy city of Vrindāban is given by Klaus Klostermaier, a Roman Catholic priest:

'Vrindāban is Krishna's paradise; only in Vrindāban can the highest degree of *prema-bhakti* be attained, as the goat-girls possessed it ... The people are Hindu in body and soul – in thought, feeling and speech ... The atmosphere is filled with the drone of drums, the tinkling of bells, and the incessant, chorus-like invocations of Krishna and Rādhā: in the temples, in the houses, on the streets, in the fields. Everything and everybody sings the praises of the divine couple ... Night and day, the praises of Krishna

and Rādhā are sung and played in Vṛindāban. Everywhere
their picture hangs, everywhere their statues stand, everywhere there is a tree, a stone, a temple, a square connected
with a particular incident in the life of Krishna. On many
an evening, there are performances of Krishna's story in
various squares in town, performed by colourfully decked
out boys in front of an ever-ecstatic public.' In his chapter,
'Indian Christmas', Klostermaier describes how his friend
Gopāljī celebrated the birthday of Krishna. Incense was
lit in his home and one after another prostrated themselves
before the small metal figure of the divine child in its robe
of yellow silk, lying on silken pillows in a silver cradle,
and touched it reverently. 'Gopāljī saw Krishna in dream
and vision, but longed to see him in reality and to serve
him eternally in heaven.' (39)

In this and the preceding section I have introduced
the reader to two particular aspects of Hinduism, the
teaching of the Gītā, and the main features of the bhakti
movements which in part developed out of it. Together
with the worship of the temples (chapter 3) and the
teaching of the Upanishads (chapter 2), they are basic
ingredients to the complex religious and social pattern of
Hinduism. Hinduism is, however, in the words of Pandit
Nehru, the first Prime Minister of independent India,
'vague, amorphous, many-sided; all things to all men. It
is hardly possible to define it, or indeed to say definitely
whether it is a religion or not, in the usual sense of the
word. In its present form, and even in the past, it embraces
many beliefs and practices, from the highest to the lowest,
often opposed to or contradicting each other.' (40)

There are many other developments within Hinduism;
its reform movements, its political aspects, and the work
of great modern teachers – Rabindranath Tagore, Mahāt-

ma Gāndhī, Dr Rādhakrishnan and Śri Aurobindo. Hindu sects have in recent years attracted interest in Britain and elsewhere. Some facets of Hinduism appear incongruous and even repellent to people of other faiths; the association of immoral acts and motives with the divine, practices associated with images and idols in the temples, the injustices of the caste system, the austerities of the ascetics and the emotional emphasis of the bhakti sects, the association of sexuality with creative power. I do not wish to minimize these elements in Hinduism, nor to claim that I have given a representative outline of the many varieties of belief and practice which are called Hindu. My aim has been, as with other religions, to enlarge our understanding of this form of belief, to explain and to identify some of the elements within Hinduism which offer material for dialogue in the search for world community.

4. *The Bread of Tomorrow*

Jesus taught that God is gracious and that he constantly seeks the well-being of his creatures. He provides food for the birds and clothing for the flowers; a sparrow cannot fall to the ground without God's knowledge and yet a human person is worth much more than a bird. He spoke often of God's banquet to which his Jewish contemporaries looked forward as a symbol of the kingdom of God at the end of history; its guests, Jesus said, are not those who thought they had a right to be invited to it, but the crippled and the lame from the backstreets, unwashed labourers from the fields, beggars, vagabonds and refugees from the highways and byways of the world. It is a banquet open not only to the Jews but to people from all four quarters of the world as well. (41)

Jesus healed and taught those who came to him, not only from cosmopolitan Galilee, but from Syria, Transjordan and Greek Decapolis as well. Towards the end of his life, after he had been temporarily accepted by the festival crowds at Jerusalem as God's chosen king of peace, he immediately took steps to secure a quiet place in the Temple for the soldiers of the occupying Roman government to say their prayers; the market which he ejected was held in the Court of the Gentiles, the only area in the temple precincts which was accessible to Gentiles, i.e. non-Jews. 'God's Temple,' he said, 'will be called a house of prayer for the people of all nations ...' (42)

Jesus' favourite way of telling of the grace of God was to speak about the kingdom of God. This was natural since the royal rule of God was a central theme in the Jewish scriptures, and the coming of his kingdom a constant preoccupation. Some Jews were content to live under Roman rule and to accommodate themselves to it, but not the majority, who longed for the rule of God to be re-established as a political reality in Jerusalem. Some, like the Zealots, tried to achieve this by force of arms, others dreamed of intervention by an agent of God, whether a descendant of the ancient royal house, a Messiah, or a supernatural being who would come on the clouds of heaven, while others, like the Pharisees, sought to bring in God's kingdom by meticulous observance of the Torah in all its detail. Jesus understood these hopes and longings, for he was a Jew, brought up in the Jewish tradition, and he stood within the tradition of the prophets of the Old Testament. Like them he proclaimed God's rule in the world.

When Jesus spoke about the coming kingdom and God's final intervention in human history, he used ideas and images which his contemporaries associated with the coming of the Son of Man, and the times of upheaval and trouble which were expected to precede the End. 'In the days after that time of trouble the sun will grow dark, the moon will no longer shine, the stars will fall from heaven, and the powers in space will be driven from their courses. Then the Son of Man will appear, coming in the clouds with great power and glory. He will send the angels out to the four corners of the earth to gather God's chosen people from one end of the world to the other.' (43)

Jesus, however, did not simply repeat teaching which was current in his time; he developed it in new ways and enriched it with his own personal insights and sensitivity. For him the kingdom of God was not some golden age postponed to a far distant time in the future, nor a kingdom for the few; the kingdom of God, as Jesus preached it and lived it, was the presence of God within the life of the world, ceaselessly active for the fulfilment of his intention for all his creatures. The Gospels make this plain in the way in which they describe the beginning of his public ministry. It was preceded by an act of committal in which Jesus accepted his vocation to be God's servant, and by a time of recollection and meditation in the desert. Returning from this time of withdrawal, 'Jesus went to Galilee,' wrote Mark, 'and preached the good news from God. "The right time has come," he said, "and the kingdom of God is near! Turn away from your sins and believe the Good News."' Luke's account is more specific. 'Jesus went to Nazareth where he had been brought up, and on the Sabbath he went as usual to the synagogue. He stood up to read the scriptures and was handed the book of the prophet Isaiah. He unrolled the scroll and found the place where it is written,

"The Spirit of the Lord is upon me, because he has chosen me to bring good news to the poor.
He has sent me to proclaim liberty to the captives and recovery of sight to the blind; to set free the oppressed and announce that the time has come when the Lord will save his people."

Jesus rolled up the scroll, gave it back to the attendant, and sat down. All the people in the synagogue had their eyes fixed on him, as he said to them, "This passage of scripture has come true today, as you heard it being read."' (44)

Jesus emphasized the imminence of God's kingdom all through his ministry; he linked it with his healing of the sick, and the comfort which he brought to the troubled and the downcast. 'It is by means of God's power that I drive out demons,' he said, 'and this proves that the kingdom of God has already come to you.' Asked when the kingdom of God would come, he answered, 'The kingdom of God does not come in such a way as to be seen. No one will say, "Look, here it is!" or, "There it is!"; because the kingdom of God is within you [or, among you].' Through his ministry, 'the Good News about the kingdom of God was being told, and everyone was forcing his way in'. (44)

These and other sayings about the imminence of the kingdom of God must be put alongside Jesus' teaching about the coming of the Son of Man. It can be stated thus: the kingdom of God and the world of men interpenetrate each other, they are intimately related to each other, but they do not coincide. The kingdom of God is the great mystery of creation which interacts with the transient life of earthly existence and constantly changes and transforms it.

God's kingdom, however, is a reality which lies hidden within human existence; it can only be discovered by those who are sensitive to its truth and its ways. 'The gate to life is narrow and the way that leads to it is hard, and there are few people who find it.' The first and last of the eight stanzas of the Beatitudes make it clear that happiness is closely linked with God's kingdom. It belongs to those 'who know their need of God' and who may suffer persecution in trying to effect God's righteous will. Jesus offered a share in God's kingdom to all who go his way, and pay the price which doing so demands. (46)

In helping his disciples to take possession of God's kingdom in the circumstances of their everyday lives and to discover God's grace afresh each day, Jesus taught them a very simple way of praying. It is summed up in the Lord's Prayer which is used every day by hundreds of millions of people all across the world. The Gospels record it in more than one version, and this variety reflects the use made of it in public worship, as well as Jesus' flexibility in teaching it to his disciples. Here it is in its simplest form:

Our Father in heaven:
May your holy name be honoured;
may your kingdom come;
may your will be done on earth as it is in heaven.
Give us today the food we need.
Forgive us the wrongs we have done, as we forgive the wrongs that others have done to us.
Do not bring us to hard testing, but keep us safe from the evil one.

Jesus' concern for the kingdom is clear both in the opening phrases, and also in the phrase, 'Give us today the food we need', which is often translated as 'give us today our daily bread'. The adjective represented by 'we need' or 'daily' is a peculiar Greek word which occurs only here in classical and Biblical Greek literature: it should probably be translated 'bread for tomorrow', and, if this is right, it is a reference to the final fulfilment of God's kingdom and the banquet which will celebrate it. Jesus is asking his disciples to pray: 'here, today, in this ordinary earthly existence, give me a foretaste of the heavenly kingdom; help me to live my earthly life as one who belongs to God's eternal kingdom and knows its power and its joy.' (47) The last phrases also refer to the kingdom and emphasize the testing which must be faced before God's kingdom becomes a reality for all mankind. Jesus insisted that those who experience God's grace must themselves show the same graciousness to others: 'there must be no limit to your goodness, as your heavenly Father's goodness knows no bounds.' (48)

Jesus himself lived by that prayer. For him, the kingdom was always present and always victorious and he affirmed this most clearly at the Last Supper. He and his disciples met in secret, in a borrowed guest chamber. The shadow of the passion lay across the meal, throwing Jesus into deep agitation of spirit, Judas went out into the night, and Peter was foolishly boastful of his ability to stand firm against any test. Yet, at that very meal, Jesus was confident of the coming of God's kingdom. Hero-like he made a vow of abstinence, declaring that he would 'drink from the fruit of the vine no more until the time when the kingdom of God comes', and he formally bestowed upon his apostles a share in that kingdom. 'You are the men,' he said, 'who have stood firmly by me in my times of trial; and now I vest in you the kingship which my Father vested in me; you shall eat and drink at my table in my kingdom and sit on thrones as judges of the twelve tribes of Israel.' It is easy for us to understand these words, for we stand on this side of the Resurrection, but in the dark tragedy of the upper room, when all was at risk and the crucifixion yet in the future, Jesus' words display a courage and trust in God which are beyond our comprehension. They enabled him to see in the breaking of the bread a sign of his victory and to climb the hill of Calvary with steadfastness and patience. The upper room was for him a foretaste of the heavenly banquet, where in the broken bread of today he tasted the bread of God's tomorrow. In the same spirit, when hanging on the cross and near to death, he prayed his evening prayer and committed his spirit into his Father's hands. (49)

We see in the words of Jesus and especially in his great prayer, his distinctive teaching about man's relationship with God. In its essence it is a simple attitude of trust and obedience, similar to that between a child and his father, and it encompasses the whole of life. Its inspiration is not to be found in mystical experience of a particular kind, nor in spiritual discipline alone, but primarily within the experiences of everyday life. It is there that men find entry into God's kingdom and by walking the path of obedience and of trust the bread of today's needs is transformed into the bread of God's final triumph. (50)

Postscript

The accounts of prayer and meditation given in this chapter illustrate the instinctive desire of human beings for communion with God. The similarities between them, noticed in the first section, arise in part from their common shared humanity but they arise also from the universal presence of the Eternal Father to whom all prayer is addressed. The great vision of God set out in the poetry of the Gītā echoes in Hindu idiom other great visions of God, for example, in the Bible and the Qur'ān.

> God is the Light of the Heavens and the Earth:
>   his light is like a lamp in a niche,
>   like a lamp in a glass, like a shining star,
>   fuelled [by oil from] a blessed tree,
>   an olive neither of the East nor of the West,
>   its oil would almost shine even if no fire were to touch
>   it –:
> God guides to his light whoever he wills: ...
> In temples God has permitted to be erected and his Name commemorated therein, with people praising him at morning and at evening ...
> Have you not seen that whatever is in the Heavens and the Earth praises him, even the birds spreading their wings?
> Each one, he knows its prayer and its praising: God knows what they do.
> To God belongs the sovereignty of the Heavens and the Earth, and to him is the home-coming. (51)

Communion, however, can become an end in itself, if the emphasis is placed too narrowly upon the salvation of the individual soul and its blessedness: the bhakti movements of Hinduism appear to run the risk of doing this without the correction of an accompanying moral purpose, but this happens in other religions also, including Christianity. By contrast, Jesus set the kingdom of God in the context of the world's life. He taught his disciples to enter into a living relationship with God by responding to his grace themselves and by seeking the transformation of society so that its common life is remade to share God's glory.

NOTES

1. See Conze, op. cit. 201–5; *Towards the Meeting with Buddhism*, II, 67–70: *A Guide to Religions*, 141.
2. Constance Padwick, *Muslim Devotions*, 48–54.
3. See William Johnston, *Silent Music*, Collins, 1974, and Fount Paperbacks, 58–60.
4. Professor Yūsuf K. Ibish, quoted in Charis Waddy, *The Muslim Mind*, 155.
5. Abhishiktananda, *Prayer*, SPCK, 1967, 39. See also Catherine de Hueck Doherty, *Poustinia*, Fount Paperbacks, 1977, 21.
6. Abhishiktananda, op. cit., 35–6.
7. R. A. Nicholson, 'Mysticism', in *The Legacy of Islam*, Oxford, 1931, 213. See also Sister Mary Paul, SLG, *Loving God for Himself Alone*, Fairacres Publication 52, Oxford, 1975.
8. Johnston, op. cit., 71–3.
9. Mark Gibbard, *Guides to Hidden Springs*, SCM, 1979, 7.
10. See Padwick, op. cit., 220–31.
11. Kenneth Cragg, *The Wisdom of the Sufis*, Sheldon Press, 1976, 16. See also the article 'Taṣawwuf' in the *Shorter Encyclopaedia of Islam*.

12. Sultanhussein Tabandeh, *A Muslim Commentary on the Universal Declaration of Human Rights*, translated F. J. Goulding, 1970, VIII–IX, also reprinted in Waddy, op. cit., 156–7.

13. See R. M. French, *The Way of a Pilgrim*, SPCK, 1972: also Abhishiktananda, op. cit., 51–63.

14. Cragg, op. cit., 17: See also Waddy, op. cit., 155.

15. Abhishiktananda, op. cit., 57–8.

16. There are many translations of the Gītā into English, and it is often included in anthologies of Hindu scriptures. (Details in chapter 2, note 16.) In this chapter I take the translation from that by W. D. P. Hill, Oxford, 1953, but I have simplified the text in some instances for easier reading and added a few comments in brackets.

17. I. 28–32, 47: 2. 30–33, 37.

18. 10. 8–11, 12, 15–22, 38–42.

19. 11. 12–13, 15–21.

20. 11. 40, 43–7.

21. See especially 12. 6–12.

22. 11. 52–5.

23. 18. 64–6.

24. See chapter 2, section 2.

25. See above pages 153: for sacrifice see *Gītā* 4. 23–33.

26. See Zaehner, *Gītā*, 36–8: Hume, *Upanishads etc.*, 23–32 (chapter 2 note 12): Mascaro, 13–20.

27. V. 13, 14: II. 15: VI. 23; translation from Hume, op. cit.

28. See Zaehner, *Gītā*, 181.

29. See Zaehner, *Hinduism*, 84–91: P. Masson-Oursel and Louise Morin, 'Mythology of Hinduism', in *New Larousse Encyclopaedia of Mythology*, Paul Hamlyn, 1968, 374–8.

30. 4. 6–8 (Parrinder's translation).

31. See O'Flaherty, *Hindu Myths*, Penguin, 1975, 235–7: Zaehner, *Hinduism*, 91.

32. e.g. O'Flaherty, op. cit.: *Encyclopaedia of Mythology*, 359–78.

33. See *Hindu Myths*, 198–204: *Encyclopaedia of Mythology*, 370–4.

34. See especially Bouquet, op. cit., 86–7.

35. See *Hindu Myths*, 204–31: *Encyclopaedia of Mythology*, 367–70: the whole saga is retold in Nigel Frith, *The Legend of Krishna*, London, Sheldon Press, 1975.

36. Zaehner, *Hinduism*, 145–6: *Encyclopaedia*, 375–8.

37. Zaehner, op. cit., 132–3: See also Bouquet, op. cit., 89–90. The first two verses are from Māṇikka Vāsagar, a Tamil devotee of Śiva in the ninth century AD.

38. Zaehner, op. cit., 127.

39. *Hindu and Christian in Vrindaban*, London, SCM, 1969.

40. Quoted in *A Guide to Religions*, 63.

41. Matthew 6. 25–34: Luke 15: Luke 14. 12–24: Matthew 8. 10–12.

42. Matthew 4. 23–5: Mark 11. 1–11, 15–19: Mark 14, 3–9.

43. Mark 13. 24–7. The sayings of Jesus about the coming of the Son of Man are difficult to interpret precisely, and the passages in the Gospels in which they occur have been edited in various ways.

44. Mark 1. 14–15: Luke 4. 16–21.

45. Luke 11. 20: 19. 9–10: 17. 20–21: 16. 16.

46. Matthew 7. 14: 5. 3, 10: 10. 38.

47. See e.g. Jeremias, op. cit., 199–201.

48. Matthew 5. 48 (NEB).

49. Luke 22. 18, 28–30 (NEB): Luke 23. 46.

50. Such a transformation is the theme of the Christian worship service of Holy Communion.
51. Q. 24. 25–6, 41–2.

CHAPTER 6

Healing

1. *The Dark Shadow*

To walk the path of communion with God is man's highest good, and source of his deepest joy. What it means to do this is described in the writings of the mystics; it is for 'the lover to be alone with his beloved', for the human person to attain 'the vision of glory of the God of all, where are beauty and victory and joy and all righteousness, and where, again and again, joy fills the soul.' (1) The last chapter examined the ways in which communion with God is taught and practised in different religions.

Human life, however, is marked by pain and suffering. There is a brokenness about our individual lives, as well as our corporate ones, which spoils our highest hopes and our deepest joys. It is as if we passed through life's experiences in the company of a dark shadow which threatens our serenity and our happiness. This is not to depreciate the joy and fulfilment which are given to us time and again; it is simply to recognize that there are also present factors which can diminish joy or turn happiness into pain and sorrow. The whole adventure of mankind has been marked by pain, failure and disappointment as well as by joy and progress.

Pain and failure touch us at many levels and in many different ways. At the personal level physical failure can overwhelm by its intensity or oppress the sufferer with continual discomfort, embarrassment or disability. Or the injury may be within the mind, hindering the development of the personality or causing the afflicted person to injure himself or others. Humans are disturbed by emotions: envy, anger, lust; or they may lack the strength of character to sustain ideals and work for them. Added to this is the certainty of death which threatens everyone with the loss of personal identity and the final failure to achieve hopes and dreams.

Suffering and pain are integral also to human existence and in people's relationships with each other, whether within a family or a community. Almost every family knows tensions and strains. In the wider community, conflicts between different groups and interests cause injustice and violence, or the exploitation of one section of society for the benefit of another. This happens also on the world scene. 'We are being given immense opportunities for the liberation and enrichment of all men. We are asked to make choices about how those opportunities will be used. Yet we seem incapable of making the right choice, the choice of life. Rather the "sin in the structures" seems constantly to make destructive choices nearly inevitable. And as the opportunities before us are immense in their potential, so are the consequences of the wrong choices in their destructiveness.' Professor Charles Elliott, in his lecture to the Lambeth Conference of 1978, went on to speak of 'the economy of death that exports 6 billion worth of arms to countries that cannot feed, clothe and house their populations'. (2)

Suffering is not confined to those who live in circumstances of poverty, or of political or social deprivation. In one way or another it is an integral part of the human condition and to be a human person is to be familiar with pain, with failure, with disappointment. No one, however privileged, escapes this dark shadow. Suffering is a concomitant of human life, associated with man's creatureliness and vulnerability.

Buddhism takes seriously the suffering and pain of the world since it was his experience of them in others which led the young Gautama Siddhārtha to forsake his home in the quest for enlightenment. Deliverance, he taught, comes by winning detachment from desire through walking the Noble Eightfold Path and thus entering the bliss of Nirvāna. (3) In one sense, Nirvāna is the extinction (literally 'the blowing out'), of life, or rather of life as we know it in earthly, transient experience, and with it the destruction of passion, delusion and craving. But in a positive sense Nirvāna is also 'a state of liberation, of spiritual freedom uninhibited by space, time, or causation'. (4)

Coupled with this quest for Nirvāna, is the Buddhist doctrine of *an-ātman*, the illusion of the self. There are, Buddhists say, five 'heaps' which, taken together, give the illusion that there is a self which holds them together: the body, feelings, perceptions, impulses and emotions, acts of consciousness. In reality, these separate sensations are distinct from each other, but they follow so fast upon one another, that they give the illusion of a self over and beyond those particular sensations. It is the illusion of a self, the 'no-soul' of transient experience, which desires and craves for this or that pleasure, which is anxious, elated or downcast and thus the cause of suffering. In Nirvāna that illusion will be no more and the true self will find its being in what alone is real. (5)

To walk the Eightfold Path which leads to an understanding of the true nature of transient experience brings deliverance from the suffering caused by the illusion of the self. But this does not in itself mean the end of suffering;

it may, in fact, increase awareness of and compassion for the suffering of the whole universe. Thus developed, in *Mahāyāna* Buddhism, belief in the *Bodhisattvas*, the saints who delay their entrance into Nirvāna in order to bring others with them into that unending bliss. The *Prajnā-pāramitā Sūtra* describes their service as follows. 'Doers of what is hard are the *Bodhisattvas*, the great beings who have set out to win supreme enlightenment. They do not wish to attain their own private Nirvāna. On the contrary, they have surveyed the highly painful world of being, and yet, desirous to win supreme enlightenment, they do not tremble at birth-and-death. They have set out for the benefit of the world, for the ease of the world, out of pity for the world. They have resolved: "We will become a shelter for the world, a refuge for the world, the world's place of rest, the final relief of the world, islands of the world, lights of the world, leaders of the world, the world's means of salvation."' (6) Associated with them are supernatural beings, embodiments of the Buddha nature, who rule celestial kingdoms and seek the salvation of all who worship them and in loving faith invoke their name. The foremost of the heavenly Buddhas is *Amitābha*, the Buddha of Infinite Light; he is a glorious saviour who inhabits a heavenly paradise, 'The Pure Land', in the west beyond the galaxies, where he sits 'on a lotus seat like a gold mountain in the midst of all its glories, surrounded by his saints'. (7) The heavenly Buddhas are recognized to be 'productions of the mind' but they personify the Buddha-reality in such a way that they are for their worshippers wholly trustworthy. (8)

Nirvāna is also a Hindu term and it describes the state of bliss into which the human soul enters when it has achieved that union with Brahman which gives deliverance from the recurring cycles of earthly existence. As we have already seen, such a state may be achieved in a variety of ways including those of devotion (bhakti) and of recollection and self-discipline (yoga). (9)

The emphasis upon human endeavour and discipline which we find in Hinduism and to an even greater extent in *Theravāda* Buddhism, which remained closer to the original teaching of the Buddha, does not, however, meet the needs of many people as they wrestle with the dark shadow lying across their path. In Hinduism prayer and sacrifice were always recognized to be one means by which a person might seek the help of the gods and begin to walk the path of deliverance. In popular Buddhism also, as it was developed at the temples containing images and relics of the Buddha, acts of worship begin with homage to the Buddha, the Three Refuges and the Five Precepts. Offerings are then presented and prayer is made that through the gifts Nirvāna may be attained and sin destroyed. In Burma a popular prayer, known as the Buddhist Common Prayer, is as follows. 'I beg leave! I beg leave! I beg leave! In order that any offence which I may have committed either by deed or by mouth or by thought may be nullified, I raise my joined hands in reverence to the forehead and worship, honour, look at and humbly pay homage to the Three Gems: the Buddha, the Law, and the Brotherhood [of monks] once, twice, three times, Lord. And because of this meritorious act of prostration may I be freed at all times from the Four States of Woe ... and quickly attain the Path, the Fruition, and the Noble Law of Nirvāna, Lord.' (10)

To pray thus for forgiveness and healing is a characteristic of religious practice all over the world, including the traditional religions. (11) Muslims and Christians no less than others do the same, but whereas Buddhism and Hinduism seek for deliverance from earthly existence and the attainment of Nirvāna, Islam and Christianity affirm God's saving intervention within the actual events of history.

2. *The Sovereign Mercy*

Islam affirms beyond all else the uniqueness and sovereignty of God; he is who he is in himself, nothing resembles him, and no person or thing can be equal to him or associated with him.

> He is God, One,
> God the Eternal,
> He did not beget nor was he begotten,
> No one is equal to him, not anything. (12)

The creed of Islam, the *shahāda*, states it quite categorically: 'There is not any god except [the one and only] God.' God, however, enters into relationships with his creation so that it is possible to affirm certain things about him. Traditionally these are summed up in the seven attributes of God:

1. God lives eternally, without beginning or ending: he lives independently of the universe.
2. God knows all things, past, present and future.
3. God can do all things.
4. All things exist as they are by the will of God.
5. God hears all sounds; yet he has no ear as men have.
6. God sees all things (even the steps of a black ant on a black stone on a dark night!); yet he has no eye as men have.

7. God gives to men the guidance which he promised to give, through the prophets, through the scriptures, and above all through the Qur'ān communicated through Muhammad, the seal of the prophets.

According to orthodox Muslim teaching, God's care for every detail and facet of the created universe is constant and unceasing. This is made clear in the classic statement of Dr 'Abdel Ḥaleem Maḥmūd, God holds in His Hand this interconnected structure [i.e. of the world] at every moment and throughout every second, for if He were to abandon anything in it for the twinkling of an eye, it would dissolve and vanish. God says:

'God holds the Heavens and the Earth lest they cease to be: should they cease to be, none would hold them in existence other than He. Surely He is All-Clement, All-forgiving.' (Q. 35. 41)

It is He who holds the birds in the sky: ...

'Have they not regarded the birds above them; spreading their wings and closing them? Naught holds them but the All-Merciful; surely He sees everything!' (Q. 67. 19)

God is the Possessor of Sovereignty. He grants it at any moment to whomsoever He wishes, and takes it back at any moment.

It is He who ordains the night and day at the sunrise and sunset, and it is He who grants life and reclaims it whenever a creature is born or dies. (See Q. 3. 26–7)

'There is no doubt that God created, determined and made the laws and set the rules: this is one thing. Maintaining it once it has been initiated is quite another matter. So, after the creation follows the maintenance, which is continuous and unending. This is the meaning of "*al-Qayyūmīyyah*", one of the attributes of God, for "*al-Qayyūm*" is one of his names, which means "the Self-Subsistent One by whom everything exists and continues to be."

'Does "maintenance" mean simply "upholding the universe"? No, it is maintaining it with care, and direction in accordance with this knowledge lest it disappear.' (13)

This is a clear and uncompromising statement of the direct control which God is believed to exercise throughout the entire universe. In such a context, pain and suffering as well as deliberate evil can be no more than things permitted by God for reasons which may be entirely unknown to man. God is under no obligation to explain or to justify either his own actions or those which he permits his creatures to perform or to suffer.

In the last resort, Muslim thinkers must simply acquiesce in the suffering of life and seek the rationale for evil choices and actions in the sovereign will of God. The traditional response of an Arabic-speaking Muslim to any piece of bad news is *mā shā'a llāh* 'it is that which God wills'.

The popular articles of belief set out by Najm al-Dīn al-Nasafī (died AD 1142), state quite categorically: 'God Most High is the creator of all actions of his creatures, whether of unbelief, of obedience or rebellion; all of them are by the will of God and his sentence and his conclusion and his decreeing.' (14) The Day of Judgement and the associated concept of God's justice are also fundamental beliefs in Islam; the question of human free will has thus aroused considerable controversy. Do human people have the ability to create their own actions, a state of affairs which would improperly associate them as creators with God, or is the intuition of freedom of choice another divine act which makes it just for God to reward or punish his creatures? Islamic theology finds it difficult to relate to each other the twin themes of responsibility and predestination, of human freedom and human power-lessness.

One consequence of Islam's emphasis on the immediate control by God of all contingent acts and events is that Muslims appear to be less aware of sinfulness as a con-tinuing attitude of rebellion than are Jews or Christians. The more common words in Islamic prayers denote wrong doing as single acts of transgression or error, with little emphasis on sin as an attitude of rebellion against God, or as a continuing state of sinfulness.

Even so it is the recognized practice (*sunna*) to pray a prayer for forgiveness between the two prostrations of the prayer-act. The Traditions say that it was Muham-mad's personal habit at this point to say either 'My Lord, forgive me, My Lord, forgive me', or the seven supplica-tions, namely, 'O God, forgive me, have mercy on me, and sustain me, and guide me aright, and restore me, and preserve me in health, and pardon me.' In every act of prayer the Muslim is reminded of the ever-present pos-sibility of straying from God's way when he recites from the Qur'ān, 'Guide us along the straight highway, the highway of those who receive your grace, not that of those who incur anger or who go astray.' (15)

Islam's teaching about God's immediate control of events also encourages optimism and confidence in man's ability to respond to divine grace and to make good. This note of optimism is very noticeable in the following state-ment about Islam. 'The Qur'ān,' it claims, 'has depicted a path which, when followed by a man, revolutionizes his whole life. It brings about a transformation in man's character and galvanizes him into action. This action takes the form of purification of the self, and then unceasing effort to establish the laws of God on earth, resulting in a new order based on truth, justice, virtue and goodness.

'Man plays a crucial role in the making of this world. He acts as God's vice-regent [*khalīfa*], his deputy and representative on earth. He is morally prepared to play this role. His success lies in playing it properly.' (16) Again in this passage we note the underlying confidence in the sovereignty of God: he has revealed his will, clearly and majestically to mankind in the Qur'ān, and it lies within man's power to respond to that kingly summons with obedience.

At the heart of Islamic religious experience are the twin concepts of repentance and mercy. 'The first brick in the palace of sincerity is faith, and the first tree to be planted in its garden is repentance, total and sincere repentance ... In a Holy Utterance (spoken by Muhammad), God Almighty says, "My servants, you make mistakes by day and night and I forgive all sins: ask my forgiveness and I will forgive you".' (17) Repentance is a constant theme in the Qur'ān as in the following verses:

Believers, turn, all of you, to God in repentance, that you may prosper.

Believers, turn to God in true repentance: it may be that your Lord will acquit you of your evil deeds and will bring you to the gardens under which rivers flow.

Say, 'Servants of God, you who have sinned against your

souls, do not despair of God's Mercy, for He forgives all sins: He is the Forgiving One, the Merciful.' (18)

Mercy is the attribute in God to which the believing Muslim may look for forgiveness. Indeed the two adjectives derived from it, usually translated, 'the merciful, the compassionate', are the two most common names given to God in Islam and occur with *Allāh* at the beginning of almost every chapter in the Qur'ān. Al-Ghazzāli (died AD IIII) describes the meaning of *al-Rahīm*, 'the Compassionate', as follows:

'God's Mercy is complete because he wishes to fulfil the needs of those in want and because He carries this out to the full. It is overall because it includes the deserving and undeserving, and it incorporates in its provisions luxuries as well as necessities. He is, indeed, the All-Merciful, the Compassionate, in the absolute sense.' (19)

The fruit of God's mercy is seen in the many bounties which enrich life, the provision of day and night, the mutual comfort of husband and wife (Q. 28. 73: 30. 21), and the deliverance from danger and calamity given to Job and other prophets, or to ordinary people in the calamities of everyday life (Q. 21. 83–4: 11. 58). 'It is He who sends down saving rain when they have lost all hope, and spreads out his mercy: He is the protector and the praiseworthy' (Q. 42. 28). Thus the word 'mercy' is used in the Qur'ān much in the same way as 'mercy' used to be used in English prayers and hymns: e.g. 'Almighty God, Father of all mercies, we thine unworthy servants do give thee most humble and hearty thanks for all thy goodness and loving kindness to us and to all men ...' or 'When all thy mercies, O my God, my rising soul surveys ...'. The crowning mercy is acceptance on the Day of Judgement and admission to the Gardens of the Blessed. 'Our Lord, you embrace everything in mercy and knowledge: so forgive those who repent and follow your way, and guard them against the punishment of Hell: bring them, Our Lord, to the Gardens of Eden.' (20) The prophet Muhammad reflected the mercy of God in his own conduct and commended it to others, as many of the Traditions testify. According to the teaching of Islam, mercy is the most characteristic way in which God exercises his sovereignty in the world, but it is nevertheless, in each particular circumstance, subordinate to his will. His actions of mercy and forgiveness depend upon the divine determination to disregard the particular sins which have been committed. Thus *al-Ghazzālī*, in discussing the divine name *al-Ghaffār*, 'the Very Forgiving One,' makes play upon the meaning of the root *al-ghafr* which means 'veiling': *al-Ghaffār* is the One who makes manifest what is noble and veils what is disgraceful. The sins (of man) are among the disgraceful things which he veils by placing a veil upon them in this world and disregarding their punishment in the hereafter ... God has promised that he will exchange good deeds for man's misdeeds so that he might cover the repulsive qualities of his sins with the reward of his good deeds when he has proved his faith.' (21)

What the Qur'ān says about the crucifixion of Jesus illustrates very clearly this close relationship between God's mercy and his sovereignty. Muhammad preached Islam at a time when Arab tribes, on the borders of Arabia or on its trade-routes, already had close links with Christians and with Jews. There are many references to them in the Qur'ān and its treatment of the story of the crucifixion of Jesus makes it easier for us to compare what Christianity and Islam teach about suffering and its healing. Three of the verses which refer to the death of Jesus are ambiguous and, according to the rules of Qur'ānic exegesis, must be interpreted in the light of more explicit statements revealed at a later time. Qur'ān 19. 33 records words which are attributed to Jesus when a baby in the cradle: 'Peace be upon me, the day I was born, and the day I die, and the day I am raised up alive'; they are similar to the words of John the Baptist earlier in the same chapter, and, if they do refer to a natural death, they are cancelled by subsequent Qur'ānic revelations. In Q. 3. 55 and 5. 117, Jesus is said to have been 'called to render account to God', but while in some instances the word used refers to God asking a man for the payment of his account at the end of his life, it may also refer to interim payments made during the course of a person's life.

The key passage in the Qur'ān which refers to the crucifixion is 4. 155–62. Even here, however, the main emphasis is on the supposed misdeeds of the Jews, and the reference to the crucifixion is subsidiary to the main argument of the passage:

Because they (the Jews) break their covenant, and disbelieve in the signs of God, and kill the prophets without just cause ... and because they say, 'We killed the Messiah, Jesus the son of Mary, the apostle of God'; (they did not kill him, nor did they crucify him, *but a resemblance was made for them*; those who dispute about it are in doubt about it (or him); they have no certain knowledge about it, but only follow conjecture; they did not kill him certainly, but God raised him to himself; God is mighty and wise. There is no one of the People of the Book but will believe in him before his death, and, on the Day of Resurrection, he will be a witness against them) and because of the wrong-doing of those who are Jews ... and because they devour the wealth of the people with what is worthless; We (i.e. God) have prepared for the unbelievers among them a painful punishment.

The interpretation of these verses hinges on the meaning of the phrase 'a resemblance was made for them' (*shubbiha lahum*). Many Muslim commentators take this to mean, '*a resemblance of Jesus* was made for them'; i.e. the Jews did not crucify Jesus himself but someone who had been made to resemble him. On the basis of this interpretation, Muslim commentators make many suggestions about the identity of the supposed substitute, including the following: one of the twelve apostles who responded to an appeal by Jesus for a volunteer and was promised the gardens of Paradise; a thirteenth apostle whom the Christians have deliberately refused to mention in the Gospels; an enemy such as Judas Iscariot. From this interpretation comes the commonly held belief that Jesus will return to this earth in order to undergo a natural death and so fulfil in a literal way the Qur'ānic statements about his death.

The most important of the early Muslim commentators, however, interpret the crucial phrase differently: '*a resemblance of the act of crucifying* was made for them'; i.e. the Jews imagined that they were crucifying Jesus, but in actual fact God rescued him from their hands and raised him to heaven. This interpretation allows different statements to be made about the suffering which Jesus actually endured; the older commentators, for example, say that he died for only three (or seven) hours, or, alternatively, that he endured no suffering at all.

If this interpretation is the correct explanation of the Qur'ānic text, the disputes and uncertainties of the Jews mentioned in this passage refer to their uncertainty about what was actually happening; i.e. 'they did not kill him with certainty', because God was doing something else with Jesus. This interpretation of the verse, although possibly the earliest, is not common in contemporary Islam, but it is gaining ground. Dr Kāmil Ḥusain who made an imaginative reconstruction of Christ's last day on earth based on the Gospel narratives, wrote: 'The idea of a substitute for Christ is a very crude way of explaining the Qur'ānic text ... No cultured Muslim believes in this nowadays. The text is taken to mean that the Jews thought they killed Christ but God raised him unto him in a way we can leave unexplained among the several mysteries which we have taken for granted on faith alone.' (22)

Some scholars have suggested that we have in the Qur'ānic story of the crucifixion an echo of the Docetic heresy which from the earliest days minimized the reality of Christ's human life and his sufferings. This Christian heresy has taken many forms and shortly before the time of Muhammad in the sixth century it again became prominent in the teaching of some Christians that the body of Christ was incorruptible, and insensible to the weakness of the flesh; he accepted suffering and death by a pure act of his will alone. Traces of this heresy may have become part of contemporary Arabian folklore about Jesus. (23) It is not, however, necessary to find connections with heretical Christian teaching, since the Qur'ānic story of the crucifixion follows a pattern which is common to its stories about other prophets.

The prophet first preaches to his people.

They reject his message, ridicule him, and in certain cases attack him with violence: Abraham's enemies, for example, plotted against him as the Jews did against Jesus.

The prophet is rescued by God from his persecutors.

His enemies are destroyed by an act of divine judgement.

Many of the prophets, according to the Qur'ān, were rescued from their enemies in a particular way, Noah by means of the Ark, Abraham by migration to the Holy Land, Lot by escaping from the city, Moses by the Exodus. It is this same pattern which underlies the story of Jesus in the Qur'ān; in his case he was delivered from his enemies by his ascension into Heaven. (24)

This pattern has added significance for Muslims because it was reproduced in the life of Muhammad himself. He also, during some seven or eight years of preaching in his home town of Mecca, suffered persecution and ridicule at the hands of his unbelieving fellow-townsmen. He was then given the opportunity to move with his followers to Medina, a town three hundred miles to the north, where he was given the position of arbiter between the tribes as God's apostle. This move to Medina, the *Hijra*, was of great political significance and the decisive turning point in his life. It gave him a position of authority and he was able during the next ten years to defeat the unbelieving Meccans and establish Islam among the Arab tribes. He did not hesitate to ascribe his victories in battle to the direct help of God, and he accepted his move to Medina and establishment there as the way of deliverance given to him by God. What migration to Palestine had been for Abraham and the Exodus for Moses, the Hijra was for Muhammad; and he believed the ascension to have been the God-given way of deliverance for Jesus the Messiah.

In the Qur'ānic story of the Cross we see once again that Islam sets the sovereignty of God over against the sinfulness of men. God circumvents evil and brings his purpose to fulfilment by the exercise of his authority: in the end his will triumphs, confounding the evildoer and vindicating those who obey him. This emphasis upon the sovereignty of God explains why the Christian story of the crucifixion is misunderstood and repudiated. 'A Muslim believes Jesus to be the righteous servant of God, and if he were to accept this story of the crucifixion it means that he would have to delete the name of Jesus from the list of the prophets.' (25)

The difference between the Qur'ān's assessment of the cross and the Christian story demonstrates a fundamental difference between the two religions. Islam teaches that God is the sovereign Lord, whose power and authority encompass all things. God simply wills a creature to be or an event to happen, and his will is directly and immediately effected: *qāla kun wa-kāna*, 'He says "be" and it comes to be.' Muslims have made every possible effort to understand the world in these terms and to articulate a coherent theology based upon them; they live by this teaching in their own lives, and they face the predicaments of life with perseverance and patience, hopeful of God's mercy. To stand by these truths is the faith of Islam.

3. *The Eternal Love*

(a) VICARIOUS SUFFERING

Like other religions, Christianity and Judaism, its pre-decessor, recognize that suffering and failure are constant elements in the life of mankind. The Old Testament scriptures recount the crises and disasters which marked the history of Israel: their slavery in Egypt and wanderings in the desert, the downfall of the kingdom in Jerusalem and the deportation to Mesopotamia. From then onwards (586 BC), the Jews only achieved one brief period of independence in Palestine until modern times. Their religious leaders, throughout this long history, faced the constant problem of reconciling the disasters which befell the nation, and the countless personal tragedies which accompanied them, with their faith in God who had chosen them to be his people. So also the New Testament: although they tell of the resurrection, the Gospels are the story of a prophet who was rejected by his people and died, forsaken by his disciples, on the gallows; the Epistles were written to small groups of Christians most of whom faced persecution of one kind or another. 'My dear friends, do not be bewildered by the fiery ordeal that is upon you, as though it were something extraordinary,' wrote the apostle Peter, 'it gives you a share in Christ's sufferings, and that is cause for joy.' (26) Jews and Christians of Bible times had to come to terms with both the suffering common to mankind, and all they had to endure as part of the community to which they belonged.

In reflecting upon these events, the writers of the Bible came to various conclusions, but all perceived a clear link between suffering and evil. In the story of the Fall, the story of Everyman, pain, suffering and death itself afflict Adam because of his disobedience, and he is excluded from the Garden where God had placed him in his state of innocence. All the biblical writers associate pain and suffering in one way or another with the sinfulness of human people and their acts of disobedience to God's will. Created to be the crown of creation, they constantly fail, both individually and corporately, to be what God calls them to be, and so they forfeit the good life which he had intended for them. (27)

Evil and suffering are taken seriously because they are in opposition to God's purposes, but this does not mean that evil is thought of as a power which exists independently of God's will. Satan, 'the prince of this world', is also a creature of God, and the time will come when the whole creation is restored to the intention of God's original design. Neither Jesus nor his apostles recognized any exact correspondence between particular experiences of suffering and particular acts of sin. 'The eighteen people who were killed when the tower fell on them at Siloam: do you imagine,' said Jesus, 'that they were more guilty than all the other people living at Jerusalem? I tell you they were not; but unless you repent, you will all of you come to the same end.' (28)

Christianity, therefore, like the Jewish faith, teaches that sinfulness is an integral element in the human condition. People do not only commit acts of sin; they are also sinful and thus liable both to do evil and to suffer its consequences. Jesus said: 'There is nothing that goes into a person from the outside which can make him ritually unclean. Rather, it is what comes out of a person that makes him unclean . . . For from the inside, from a person's heart, come the evil ideas which lead him to do immoral things, to rob, kill, commit adultery, be greedy, and do all sorts of evil things; deceit, indecency, jealousy, slander, pride and folly – all these evil things come from inside a person and make him unclean.'

Jesus called his contemporaries to repentance, including those who were considered righteous: 'I assure you,' he said, 'that unless you change and become like children – [dependent upon God's grace] – you will never enter the kingdom of heaven.' His teaching is consistent with that of the Jewish scriptures as expressed, for example, in some of the psalms of penitence, or by the prophet Jeremiah: 'Who can understand the human heart? There is nothing else so deceitful; it is too sick to be healed.' 'Man's thoughts and inclinations were always to evil'; only the renewal of his inner self, a 'new heart', could save him. (29)

We have referred already to the three parables in which Jesus answered the complaint of the Pharisees that he welcomed the irreligious and enjoyed fellowship with them. Each of them describes a relationship between God and human people which expresses God's concern for them and his empathy with them despite their sinfulness. God, Jesus taught, is like the shepherd who risks his life to search for a lost sheep; he is like the careful housewife who turns her whole house upside down to find a silver trinket; he is like a father who watches anxiously for a wayward son to return home, and then, when he does so, is so over-come with joy that he throws dignity to the winds and gives him a party. These pictures of God's active concern are in marked contrast to the serenity of *Nirvāna* or the sovereign mercy of Islam. (30)

These words of Jesus bear the marks of his own insight

and creative thinking, but they have their roots in the Old Testament. The prophets made much of God's sovereignty, and his kingship was a central theme in the worship at the Jerusalem Temple, but the relationship between God and Israel was conceived in more personal ways as well. God was father, not only to the king who was his vice-regent, but to Israel as well. (31) It was a personal relationship, like that between husband and wife.

So in rebuking Israel for apostasy, rebellion and injustice, the prophets emphasized the pain which estranged relationships brought to both sides, to God as well as to his people. They did not hesitate to speak of a divine love which knew what it was to be broken and sorrowful:

> The Lord said,
> 'Earth and sky listen to what I am saying!
> The children I brought up have rebelled against me.
> Cattle know who owns them, and donkeys know where their master feeds them.
> But that is more than my people Israel know. They don't understand at all.'

> The Lord says,
> 'Israel, I wanted to accept you as my son
> and give you a delightful land,
> the most beautiful land in all the world.
> I wanted you to call me father,
> and never again turn away from me.
> But like an unfaithful wife,
> You have been unfaithful to me.' (32)

In words such as these, the prophets declared that Israel's continuing rebellion and sin caused God sorrow and distress. Further thought led them to perceive that suffering may voluntarily be accepted on behalf of another. They learned this out of their own experience as they struggled to speak God's word to their nation; since the word spoke of rebuke and judgement it often caused them to suffer loneliness and even physical maltreatment. To be a faithful prophet was a task which brought with it unpopularity, abuse and sometimes death.

This was particularly true of the prophet Jeremiah. During his long ministry of nearly fifty years, he risked his life many times, suffering arrest and imprisonment as well as abuse and hostility from those who thought him a traitor to his people. Above all he suffered an inner agony, resenting at times the burden laid upon him of speaking the truth in God's name, yet torn between his love for his people and his duty towards God. 'What an unhappy man I am! Why did my mother bring me into the world? I have to quarrel and argue with everyone in the land. I have not lent any money or borrowed any: yet everyone curses me ... Remember that it is for your sake that I am insulted. You spoke to me, and I listened to every word. I belong to you, Lord God Almighty, and so your words filled my heart with joy and happiness. I did not spend my time with other people, laughing and having a good time. In obedience to your orders I stayed by myself and was filled with anger. Why do I keep on suffering? Why are my wounds incurable? Why won't they heal? Do you intend to disappoint me like a stream that goes dry in the summer?' (33)

But despite his anguish, Jeremiah could not avoid his commission to be God's prophet: 'Lord I am ridiculed and scorned all the time because I proclaim your message. But when I say, "I will forget the Lord and no longer speak his name", then your message is like a fire burning deep within me. I try my best to hold it in, but can no longer keep it back.' (34)

Jeremiah's ministry as a prophet caused him much pain, and he suffered both physically and mentally because of his faithfulness to God's call. But his persistence and courage bore fruit. He enabled others also to continue faithful in the worship of God and by so doing kept true faith alive among his people.

His example fired the imagination of an anonymous prophet who preached in Israel some thirty years after Jeremiah's ministry. His preaching is recorded in the last part of the book Isaiah; it was addressed to the people of Israel during the period when the Persians were conquering the empire of Babylon. He included among his prophecies four poems about the ministry of the one whom he called 'God's servant'; it is likely that in the fourth of these poems he had Jeremiah in mind.

> He had no dignity or beauty to make us take notice of him.
> There was nothing attractive about him.
> Nothing that would draw us to him.
> We despised and rejected him;
> he endured suffering and pain.
> No one would even look at him –
> we ignored him as if he were nothing.
> But he endured the suffering that should have been ours,
> the pain that we should have borne.
> All the while we thought that his suffering
> was punishment sent by God.
> But because of our sins he was wounded,
> beaten because of the evil we did.
> We are healed by the punishment he suffered,

made whole by the blows he received ...
The Lord says,
'It was my will that he should suffer;
his death was a sacrifice to bring forgiveness.
And so he will see his descendants;
he will live a long life,
and through him my purpose will succeed.
After a life of suffering, he will again have joy;
he will know that he did not suffer in vain ...' (35)

The unknown prophet realized that Jeremiah's suffering had borne fruit in the nation's life; he had led his countrymen towards repentance and forgiveness and enabled them to bear witness once again to God's kingship in the world. Because one servant of God had suffered willingly on behalf of others the whole Jewish nation had been strengthened to make God known to the world.

The concept of vicarious suffering leads directly to the Christian understanding of the significance of the death of Jesus. In the Middle East, as in Africa, a servant was closely identified with his master, and the words of Jesus himself illustrate this: 'Whoever welcomes you,' he said to his disciples, 'welcomes me; and whoever welcomes me welcomes the one who sent me.' God was closely involved in the suffering of his servant; in calling him to the path of suffering for the healing of mankind, God went along that road himself. (36)

(b) GOD WAS IN CHRIST

The story of the passion, death and resurrection of Jesus forms a major section in each of the four Gospels. (37)

At first sight, it is a story similar to those of other human beings like Jeremiah who have struggled with conflict and disappointment, or whose leadership has been rejected by those whom they have tried to serve. Not all have died so cruel a death as crucifixion, but they have all tasted a similar bitterness of rejection. In a strange way, however, the story of Jesus is different from those which might be compared with it and certain features make it unique, even as a purely human story. First, the suffering of Jesus was totally undeserved. He had given himself to others generously and unsparingly; without a home of his own, he had travelled throughout Galilee and beyond, teaching the multitudes who thronged and jostled him, healing the many sick who were brought to him. Secondly, he bore himself throughout his passion and crucifixion without a trace of self-pity or of resentment towards his enemies. He kept his attention on the needs of those who were close to him and continued to minister to them. Even as the nails were being driven into his hands and feet, Jesus kept saying, 'Forgive them, Father! They don't know what they are doing.' Thirdly, there is a strange but marked contrast between the use of God's power which Jesus exercised in healing others and his own helplessness when caught up as a victim in the evil purposes of others. Moreover Jesus experienced in himself a strong inner tension which showed itself in a 'deep agitation of spirit'. This distress was private to Jesus, and it went far beyond the ability of the disciples to help him. But, at the last, the tension was relieved and Jesus commended himself to God in the habitual trust of his daily prayers: 'Father! In your hands I place my spirit.' (38)

Although what we call 'the passion story' began on Palm Sunday and ended only seven days later, the suffering of

Jesus cast its shadow a long way ahead. He aroused opposition from the Pharisees and other Jewish religious leaders very early in his ministry and he warned his disciples that he might be taken from them. The crowds, who followed him at first, did not long continue with him and when his close personal friends declared their acceptance of him as God's chosen Messiah, he told them that this meant for him suffering, rejection and death. From his baptism onwards, Jesus interpreted his God-given mission in the light of prophets like Jeremiah who had suffered pain, injustice and humiliation in order to rescue their people from the consequences of their wrong-doing. Jesus said that he had come as God's servant, 'not to be served but to serve, and to give his life to redeem many people' – i.e. to liberate them from the power of evil. (39) Thus the passion of Jesus was not an isolated tragedy which occurred by chance at the end of his life; rather it was of a piece with the whole of his ministry. He lived in the hope of God's kingdom, but, from the beginning, he knew that as God's servant he would be called to vicarious suffering, to walk the path of suffering and humiliation on account of his people's sins and for their healing.

After the resurrection, when Christ's apostles told his story to the people of their day, further to the question: 'Who is Jesus?', they had to answer 'Why did he die?' They used a variety of analogies and illustrations in order to explain the purpose and meaning of the death of Jesus, drawing them from contemporary beliefs and practices. They said, for example, that his death was the perfect *sacrifice* by which sin had been expiated and people restored to a right relationship with God; this explanation appealed both to Jews who were familiar with the Old Testament and to Gentiles who knew the practices in

Greek and Roman temples. They said also that the death of Christ was *a ransom price* paid to liberate men from the consequences and power of evil; again this explanation would have appealed both to Jews and, perhaps especially, to Gentiles, who were familiar with the freeing of slaves performed as a charitable act of worship in the temples. Another explanation suggested that the death of Christ was *a cosmic conflict* in which Christ, the divine Lord, defeated the demonic powers of evil, rather in the way which the Hindu avatārs, Rāma and Krishna, are said to have done. (40)

These analogies are widely used to explain the significance of the death of Christ, and the ideas and words associated with them are used and treasured in prayers and hymns. They do not, however, do full justice to Christian belief in Christ as the divine Word made man, nor to the close involvement of God in the ministry of his Servant. The deepest insights of the apostles, therefore, went beyond the ideas associated with sacrifice and ransom, to assert that God himself was deeply involved in the suffering of Christ, his Word and his Servant.

'When anyone is joined to Christ,' wrote the apostle Paul, 'he is a new being; the old is gone, the new has come. All this is done by God, who through Christ changed us from enemies into his friends and gave us the task of making others his friends also. Our message is that *God was in Christ making all mankind his friends*. God did not keep an account of their sins, and he has given us the message which tells how he makes them his friends. Here we are, then, speaking for Christ, as though God himself were making his appeal through us. We plead on Christ's behalf: let God change you from enemies into his friends! Christ was without sin, but for our sake God made him share our sin in order that in union with him we might share the righteousness of God.'

John also, who spoke of Christ as 'the only Son who made God known' (see page 100), associated God's love with the death of Christ when he wrote: 'Dear friends, let us love one another, because love comes from God. Whoever loves is a child of God and knows God. Whoever does not love does not know God, for God is love. And God showed his love for us by sending his only Son into the world, so that we might have life through him. This is what love is: it is not that we have loved God, but that he loved us and sent his Son to be the means by which our sins are forgiven ... God is love, and whoever lives in love lives in union with God and God lives in union with him.' In a third New Testament book, the book of Revelation, the writer records a vision in which he saw in the centre of the throne of God, 'a Lamb standing with the marks of slaughter upon him'. The vision is a strange one, but the implications are clear: the suffering of Christ, the sacrificial lamb, at Calvary involves the divine Being who is at the heart of the universe. (41)

These three statements have to be set alongside other New Testament explanations of the significance of Christ's passion, and their meaning is more implicit than explicit. It is developed, profoundly but simply, by David Livingstone, the great traveller who died in Africa searching for the headwaters of the Nile. He wrote in his journal during his last year of travel: 'What is the atonement of Christ? It is himself. It is the inherent and everlasting mercy of God made apparent to human eyes and ears. The everlasting love was disclosed by our Lord's life and death. It showed that God forgives because He loves to forgive.

He works by smiles if possible; if not, by frowns. Pain is only a means of enforcing love.' (42)

Christians believe that Jesus was the Word of God, and that his death as well as his life revealed God to men. In their judgement, the selfless, persevering, gentle but strong love which Jesus gave to his contemporaries in his passion, was a translation of the love of God into the language of a human life. The love of Jesus for Peter, for the soldiers, for the dying thief, and for Judas, led his disciples to believe that God searches for his creatures, loves them in their waywardness and rebellion, and does not rest until he has won their whole-hearted allegiance to his kingdom.

This is the distinctive teaching of Christianity. Buddhism teaches that evil and suffering are temporary phenomena only, associated with man's transient earthly existence, and Islam would wish to deal with its consequences by the sovereign mercy of God. Christianity, however, asserts that God takes upon himself the burdens imposed by the presence of evil upon his creation, and in so doing neutralizes the dark shadow and transforms it into good. We cannot, as God does, see the whole saga of the universe from its beginning to its end, but we dare to hope that in the end we shall come to see that God's love is universally triumphant.

Christians believe that the passion of Jesus makes it possible for people to come to terms with evil and suffering, not only in human lives but in the whole universe. Evil and suffering are not minimized but rather seen for what they really are, hostility to the good which God purposes for his creation. And they are overcome by the action of God, who suffers with his creation in its struggle with evil and bears its pain and hostility himself. By so doing he weaves evil into his own purpose and transforms it into good. So in the end his creatures are freed from the crippling constraints of evil to grow into maturity as they reflect the goodness of God. The story of the passion and the crucifixion is not the end of the Gospel; it is for Christians the beginning of the story of God's new humanity which he brought into being through the incarnation, passion and resurrection of Jesus Christ. By the power of his love, which knows no limit and no condition, he transformed death into life, defeat into victory, evil into good; the food of today becomes for those who share that love a foretaste of the banquet of God's tomorrow.

NOTES

1. See above page 142: *Gītā*, 18. 77–8 (following Mascaro's translation).
2. Lecture given on 25th July 1978, 'Economics and Choice: The Crucial Battleground'.
3. See chapter 2, section 5.
4. See Zaehner, *Gītā*, 213–14: *Buddhist Scriptures*, 156–157.
5. *A Guide to Religions*, 131: *Buddhist Scriptures*, 151.
6. Conze, op. cit., 128.
7. *Buddhist Scriptures*, 232–6.
8. See Conze, op. cit., 149–51: *Towards the Meeting with Buddhism*, II, 8–9.
9. See chapter 2, section 2, and chapter 5, sections 2 and 3.
10. *A Guide to Religions*, 147–8.

11. See e.g. J. V. Taylor, op. cit., chapter 12.

12. Q. 112.

13. 'Abdel Ḥaleem Maḥmūd, *The Creed of Islam*, London, World of Islam Festival Trust, 1978, 27–9. Dr Maḥmūd was formerly Grand Shaikh of the al-Azhar University in Cairo.

14. From D. B. Macdonald, *Development of Muslim Theology, etc.*, 310.

15. See Constance Padwick, *Muslim Devotions*, 173–208: Q. 1.6–7.

16. The leaflet is reproduced in *Man's Religious Quest*, edited by Whitfield Foy, London, Croom Helm, in association with the Open University Press, 1978, 529–535.

17. Dr Maḥmūd, op. cit., 60.

18. Q. 24.31: 66.8: 39.53.

19. Op. cit., 74–5.

20. Q. 40.7–8.

21. Quoted in *Man's Religious Quest*, 502–3.

22. Dr Kāmil Ḥusain, *The City of Wrong*, translated by Kenneth Cragg, London, Bles, 1959, 222.

23. See G. Parrinder, *Jesus in the Qur'ān*, London, Sheldon Press, 1965, 109 ff., and J. W. Sweetman, *Islam and Christian Theology*, Lutterworth, 1945, volume 1, 79 f.

24. e.g. Q. 7. 59 ff: 11.25 ff: 21. 51–73.

25. M. Dīn, an Aḥmadīya writer, quoted in *Jesus in the Qur'ān*, 120.

26. 1 Peter 4. 12–13 (NEB).

27. Genesis 2. 4–3: See also O. A. Piper, 'Suffering and Evil', in the *Interpreter's Dictionary of the Bible*, New York, Abingdon, 1962.

28. Luke 13. 4–5.

29. Mark 7. 14–23: Luke 18. 9–14 and Matthew 18. 3: Psalm 51: Jeremiah 17. 9: Genesis 6. 5: Ezekiel 18. 31.
30. Luke 15.
31. See 2 Samuel 7. 12–16: Psalm 89. 26–7.
32. Isaiah 1. 2–3: Jeremiah 3. 19–20.
33. Jeremiah 15. 10–18.
34. 20. 8–9.
35. Isaiah 53. 2–5 and 10–11.
36. Matthew 10. 40.
37. See Matthew 21–8: Mark 11–16: Luke 19–24: John 12–21.
38. Luke 23. 34: John 13. 21 (NEB): Luke 23. 46.
39. Mark 2. 1–20 and 3. 6: John 6. 60–71: Mark 8. 27–38: 10. 45.
40. Details will be found in Christian books of theology: a summary in *A Guide to Religions*, 161–3.
41. 2 Corinthians 5. 17–21: 1 John 4. 7–19: Revelation 5. 6 (NEB).
42. J. L. MacNair, *Livingstone's Travels*, London, Dent, 1954, 378–9.

CHAPTER 7

All Their Splendour

1. *Prayer*

My own experience of prayer has been and continues to
be within Christianity but it has been enriched by contact
with other faiths, principally with Islam. First in London
and then in the Middle East I have been privileged to live
in close contact with Muslims and to have been taught
by them. Sitting in the libraries of Khartoum and Amman
Universities, on most days of each week during a year and
a half, surrounded by the great literary achievements of
Muslim scholars in theology, philosophy, law and history,
I became aware of the deep springs of faith, wisdom and
prayer within Islam.

During those years my religious experience and prayers
were deeply enriched by Islam's assertion of the sovereignty of God, a gentle but overwhelming sovereignty
which touches men and women at every point in their lives:
by the five-times-daily practice of prayer, and the moral
disciplines and neighbourliness of the yearly fast in
Ramaḍān; and by the deep stability of Islamic society,
marked by fortitude, restraint and dignity, which I am
grieved to see perverted in some Muslim countries today.
My understanding of the place of religion in society was
also profoundly changed by the wholeness of the Islamic
view which sees every area of life, personal and communal,
within God's sovereignty.

I have been privileged also to live in Africa and to visit

different parts of it. Modern scholars and anthropologists have given us a deeper understanding of the traditional religions, and their insights have come as an enrichment to me. Through them I have learnt to be more sensitive to God's presence in the whole life of the world, in the rhythms of nature and the ongoing life of the community, and to appreciate the deep, often unconscious, bonds which bind people together 'in the whole bundle of life' of their family. The Primal Vision can be of benefit to us all, not least to those who live in the fragmented societies of the Western nations.

I have come more recently to the study of Hinduism and Buddhism, but in them also I see a search for God and an awareness of communion with him which challenges me to deepen my own shallow prayers and aspirations. Christian worship can often be casual and familiar. We would gain much from learning the disciplines which are necessary for growth towards mature spirituality; perhaps also we need to learn afresh the awesome mystery of the Eternal, the Ground of all Being, and to remember that we stand at one point only on the shore of an ocean which is beyond our knowledge.

I welcome, therefore, the many different witnesses to the mystery of God which grow out of the diverse religious experience of mankind and particularly out of prayer. Each one illuminates a different facet in the relationship of God with his creation. There is a harmony between the different descriptions of God's being and nature which grow out of worship, rather than out of speculation, which I can only explain on the supposition that they describe the same living reality; and at the same time there is an authentic freshness about each particular description which comes from the particular circumstances in which it is made. In reading such a hymn of praise as that which Arjuna makes in the Gītā, or doxologies in the Qur'ān, or poems of the Jewish prophets like Amos or the unknown author of Second Isaiah, I recognize the presence of him whom Jesus called 'Our Father in Heaven'. And, in a strange way, I sense that presence also, implicit but not expressed, in reading the Buddhist classic, the *Dhammapada*. Many others besides Christians could make the following prayer their own:

'What can I say to you, my God? Shall I collect together all the words that praise your holy Name? Shall I give you all the names of this world, you, the Unnamable? Shall I call you "God of my life, meaning of my existence, hallowing of my acts, my journey's end, bitterness of my bitter hours, home of my loneliness, you my most treasured happiness"? Shall I say: "Creator, Sustainer, Pardoner, Near One, Distant One, Incomprehensible One, God both of flowers and stars, God of the gentle wind and of terrible battles, Wisdom, Power, Loyalty and Truthfulness, Eternity and Infinity, you the All-merciful, you the Just One, you Love itself"?' (1)

The wonder of God's relationship with his creation is that his relationship with each separate part is complete in itself. The tiniest fragment of his creation, a flower or a garden bird, a pebble or a grain of sand, sums up in itself the long processes of evolution, and exhibits the same characteristics which mark the whole creation in its relationship with God, the transcendent ground of its being and source of its life; dependence, stability, purpose and self-identity. In the same way, every human person represents in himself or herself the history of mankind in its relationship with God in all its tragedy and its glory. To be sure, we can only be fully developed human persons in relationship with others; nevertheless God is present to each separate person, however lowly, with his whole love and his whole grace. This divine presence confers dignity and value on every human, and invests each person's prayer with significance. In using the word 'prayer', I mean the whole vast activity of praise, adoration, meditation and petition by which men and women express their dependence upon God and respond to him. The response may be individual or corporate, expressed in the privacy of an inner room, in a public place, or in a building set apart for worship. In this wide sense, prayer is one of the most characteristic of all human activities. It is plain, however, that because of his love, God does not compel either our attention or our obedience.

Just as there is a basic core of awareness common to all that the different religions say about God, so there is in their varying practices of prayer. The fundamental attitudes are similar, even though the outward postures or the words used may differ from one religion to another. Praise, awe, dependence, trust and petition are ingredients common to all the responses which people make to the presence of the transcendent. At sowing or at harvest, in times of sickness or of natural disaster, before battle or at the beginning of a hunt, at the launching of a ship or an expedition, at the installation of a new government or the coronation of a monarch, in times of crisis or of victory, on these occasions communities turn naturally to prayer. They have their counterparts in the lives of families and individuals: times of sickness or danger, at birth and death, when couples are married or young people come to adulthood. These occasions awaken men and women to perceive the presence with them of a power and a purpose beyond their own and to respond accordingly.

It is often suggested, in line with the secularist attitudes of our time, that the religious interpretation of the world and man's place within it, as creatures dependent upon the will and purpose of a transcendent being, is not only inappropriate and untrue, but can also prevent mankind from using the opportunities which science and technology present for future development. There is, of course, an obligation upon religious thinkers to respond to the new perspectives introduced by science, and theology in all the religions needs to be set free from scholastic preoccupation with the past and expressed in fresh and contemporary ways. But to say that does not deny the contribution which theology has always made in enabling people to speak about the universe in universal terms. The transcendent mysteries of our human existence cannot be domesticated or tamed; they will always continue to demand response, and that is the basis of worship.

2. *Jesus Christ*

While I understand a little about other faiths, particularly Islam, I remain a Christian. In part this is because I was born into a Christian family and grew up in a Christian environment, but not entirely so. I am glad to be a Christian not only because it is the religion of my community but even more because I find in Christ, and in my discipleship to him within the Church, the means of entering into a deep and life-sustaining relationship with God.

Jesus is the strong yet gentle leader whom I desire to follow. He is for me the one person in the whole life of the world whose friendship I most covet, and the person in whom I see most clearly the marks of God's presence.

I hear in his words and see in the stories which are told about him the truth by which I need to live. And I discover, as I try to live by it, that it corresponds to the pattern of things as they exist in the universe. This is, of course, a personal affirmation, which many would find difficult to share, especially those who are devoted to the Buddha or to one of the Hindu avatārs, Rāma or Krishna, or for whom Muhammad is 'the seal of the prophets'. There are also, however, particular aspects of the Christian faith which are for me cogent reasons why I believe the Good News of Christ provides the means by which the diverse religions of mankind may be reconciled with one another.

In the first place, Christianity accepts the whole story of mankind's history within the universe, not yet ended, as a particular area in which God's presence is disclosed and his gift of salvation received and enjoyed. This emphasis on history as the sphere of God's activity is in contrast with the search for Nirvāna which is integral to Buddhism, and, in a different way, with the Hindu quest for the realization of the unity between the individual human soul and Brahman.

Secondly, the Way, which was taught and lived by Christ, offers hope to the human family in its journey towards Tomorrow. To walk his way is to discover God's kingdom within the circumstances of everyday life (chapter 5 (4)), and, by responding to God's generous grace, to live as citizens of it (chapter 5 (4)). His way offers a style of responsible openness towards others, of concern for justice and peace, and of dependence upon the resources of God's kingdom, which enables human people to become the 'Good Persons' needed to cope with the opportunities and crises of our time.

Thirdly, the story of the passion reveals the divine love as a dynamic power which transforms human existence. The love of God revealed in Christ is different from the sovereign mercy of which Islam speaks (chapter 6 (2)). It is similar in some ways to the vicarious love associated with the *Bodhisattvas* (see page 180), but again basically different in that it changes existing situations of darkness into light, of despair into hope. The passion, death and resurrection of Jesus are unique to Christianity and they declare a way by which people may find the power to master disappointment and failure and transform them into good. This appears to be in line with the pattern of growth in the natural universe as well, where the decline or failure of one system or species often provides a stepping-stone for new development and growth.

Faith in Jesus Christ, however, should not deter his followers from the task of understanding other religions, listening to their testimonies about the living God, and entering into dialogue with their neighbours who practise them. As I pointed out in the Introduction, there are many indications throughout the whole biblical tradition that 'the others', those who are neither Jews (in the Old Testament) nor Christians (in the New Testament), are themselves beloved of God, recipients of his grace, and worthy, therefore, of respect and consideration. To develop this theme in detail would be out of place in this book, and I can only indicate some of the main strands in this aspect of the tradition.

'The nations' are an important element in the Bible writers' understanding of history: not only were they dispersed and settled according to God's will, and answerable to him, but they would also be brought to share in the consummation of God's purposes for his creation: the great vision of the End in the last book of the Bible indeed declares that 'the greatness and the wealth of the nations will be brought into God's city'. (2) The final hope is that 'the dwelling of God will be with men. He will dwell with them and they shall be his peoples' (*peoples*, not *people*, is probably the original reading). (3) It is generally recognized also that the effective agents of God's will in the world, variously called Spirit, Wisdom and Word, are active throughout the whole of creation: the Spirit brings order out of primeval chaos, Wisdom is active wherever kings rule justly, 'the Word was the real light that comes into the world and shines on all mankind'. (4) In the Acts of the Apostles, the baptism of Cornelius, a Roman army officer, and Peter's vision which endorsed it, were of crucial importance in helping the Church become a universal community: this theme is taken up again in Paul's speech at Athens to the Greek philosophers when he declared the presence and care of God for all mankind. As the letters to the Colossians and Ephesians put it, God's plan is 'to reconcile the whole universe to himself, to bring all creation together, everything in heaven and on earth, with Christ as head'. (5) The first Christians recognized the Jewish experience of God's grace throughout Israel's history. It was not only the prelude to the new covenant in Christ, but also itself an authentic relationship with God from which Christians could learn.

Christians believe that in Jesus God's Word became incarnate within the whole life of mankind. This is expressed symbolically in the title of 'the second Adam' which was given to Christ by St Paul and in the genealogy of Luke's Gospel in which the first human ancestors of Jesus are listed as 'the son of Seth, the son of Adam, the son of God'. (6) Jesus was not heir only to the Jewish faith and to the Torah. Many years before he was born, the Buddha had received 'enlightenment', and Confucius and the Taoist fathers, as well as Socrates and the other Greek philosophers, had already given their wisdom to the world. Islam alone of the world's great religions had not yet been preached by Muhammad, but the seeds of its later development were already present in the Semitic prophets. The Word became man in Jesus and thereby entered into a new human relationship with the whole diverse life of mankind, in which God had already made himself known, through his Word, in many different ways.

There are, as this section indicates, two different, and apparently contradictory, obligations upon Christians in respect of people of other faiths. One obligation is to make Christ known as Lord and Saviour and to invite others to become his disciples, the other is to listen with sympathy to what others have to say about God's grace as it has become known to them. To fulfil both obligations is a task calling for great sensitivity, but it is one which people of other faiths also have to undertake in speaking about their faith with Christians. This mutual testimony is a basic principle of dialogue.

The strongest impetus for dialogue comes from a consideration of the teaching and ministry of Jesus himself. The kingdom of God is the generous gift of God, accessible and open to all those who are willing to receive it. Jesus proclaimed this kingdom, not in the holy city of Jerusalem where access to the inner courts of the Temple was denied to all who were not Jews, but on a hillside in Galilee of the Gentiles where the population was much more mixed. It was from there, according to one tradition (7), that he sent his disciples to take the good news of God's kingdom to all the nations. He spoke also of 'other sheep which belonged to him that are not in this sheepfold' whom he would bring to become one flock with one shepherd. He gave his life, 'not only for the Jewish people, but also to bring together into one body all the scattered people of God'. The Church's task is to continue the reconciliation which Jesus sought and to do it his way: with generosity and with gentleness, counting it a far greater privilege to give than to get. This is the only effective style for dialogue and it is appropriate for people of all faiths to follow. (8)

3. *The End*

Together with people of other faiths, I believe that God reigns as sovereign in the long history of the universe and that he is working towards an End which will fulfil his purpose in creation and for mankind. I cannot imagine that End, but I can identify certain elements which I hope will find a place within it.

The End, I hope, will be one to which all the different religions will make particular contributions. All that has been learnt about God and his relationship with the world, all that has been discovered and affirmed of beauty, truth and goodness, will not be lost but gathered into God's kingdom.

The ultimate frontier is none of those which men now guard to separate one group from another, but that which has always existed between the material world and the transcendent, between the contingent and the eternal, between man and God. This frontier unites mankind because all men live on the same side of it. To stand together in this way is to be united in a common humanity, and to face a common destiny. Face to face with the living God, we reflect his glory and receive his grace: united in that way we can build the earth as his children. The difficulties are real, and men are divided by religion as much as they are by race or politics, but God is one, and in his presence we can learn to speak a common language. It is a language which we need to speak if we are to build a world community securely and in truth; to achieve a harmony within the infinitely varied life of mankind demands a constant and sustained effort at dialogue between those who differ from each other, in religion as much as in other areas of life.

In this book we have explored together five themes which are common in various ways to all the religions.

Human people live in the presence of a transcendent reality upon which or upon whom they depend for fulness of life: chapter 2.

God's word is addressed to them through the natural universe, the words of the prophets and the scriptures: chapter 3.

People are called to live in ways which are congruent with God's word, or grow out of the nature of the universe, the way things are: chapter 4.

Prayer and worship are ways by which people may enter into communion with the transcendent: chapter 5.

Religious faith and worship offer means by which evil may be overcome and suffering be healed: chapter 6.

There are many differences between the ways in which the different religions work out these themes, and certainly this summary does not do justice to any single one of them, least of all to the Christian Gospel as I outlined it in the previous section. Nevertheless it represents some common ground, the headings of an agenda on the basis of which meaningful dialogue can take place.

The analogy of the electric grid, to which I referred in chapter 1, suggests that each religion must contribute to the whole life of mankind from its own treasures and resources. Particular contributions will be made by different religions; we need them all if the human community is to grow towards a harmonious plural community. The contributions will be many and various; they will include the disciplined moderation and gentleness of the Buddhist path with its veneration for all living creatures, Hinduism's awareness of the self and quest for reality, the disciplined prayer life of Islam with its accompanying duties of almsgiving and of fasting and self-denial, and the joy of Judaism in the living-out of God's Law. Included also will be the wisdom of the Chinese and the healing, victorious power of Christ's passion. As we look towards the building of a harmonious world-community we need the rich diversity of religious experience to inspire and to challenge us. Only so will we become the kind of people who can cope with the demands which such a world-community will make upon us, and who can use its opportunity to the full.

The prophet John was given a vision of the universal city at the end of history: 'The street of the city was of pure gold, transparent as glass. I did not see a temple in the city, because its temple is the Lord God Almighty and the Lamb. The city has no need of the sun or the moon to shine on it, because the glory of God shines on it, and the Lamb is its lamp. The peoples of the world will walk by its light, and the kings of the earth will bring into it all their splendour. The gates of the city will stand open all day; they will never be closed, because there will be no night there. The greatness and the wealth of the nations will be brought into the city. But nothing that is impure will enter the city, nor anyone who does shameful things or tells lies.' (9)

That is the universal city of men's dreams: it is one into which all may enter without hindrance through open gates, and, bringing their treasures with them, contribute to its wealth.

I believe also that, in a way which we cannot now perceive, Christ will provide the link by which the different religions will be brought into a deep and mutually enriching relationship with each other. That may appear an insensitive thing to write at the end of a book like this but it is a Christian hope as old as Christ himself who, as the Good Shepherd, longed to bring people of different folds into one flock. The apostle Paul declared his hope that God would one day 'put his hidden purpose into effect and bring the universe, all in heaven and on earth, into a unity in Christ', and, in his great vision, John saw the universal city lit by the glory of God in and through Christ. (10) There is much theological work to be done and many generations of dialogue before such a hope can ever come to fruition: but the task is a priority to which the churches must now give their attention.

Lastly, I believe that the End is in God's hands, and that it will completely transcend anything that we can imagine. It will be a human community marked by rich diversity and universal harmony: it will reach beyond space and time into Eternity.

Meanwhile, as we hope for tomorrow, there are today things for us all to do, to whatever faith we belong, in preparation for it.

We are called to be faithful in our personal discipleship, sharing with others what God has given to us of his grace and his truth.

We are called to reach out towards people of other faiths in mutual understanding and a responsible dialogue which is grounded in the realities of community relationships.

We are called to build our pluralist communities together in justice, in peace and in truth.

We go on in hope because God will be at the End as he was at the Beginning.

NOTES

1. Karl Rahner, *Prayers for Meditation*, quoted in Kenneth Cragg, *Alive to God*, Oxford, 1970, 63.
2. Deuteronomy 33. 8: Amos 1–2: Revelation 21. 26.
3. See J. Sweet, *Revelation*, SCM Press, 1979, on Revelation 21. 3.
4. Genesis 1. 1–2: Proverbs 8. 15–16: John 1. 9.
5. Acts 10: 17. 16–34: Colossians 1.20: Ephesians 1. 10.
6. 1 Corinthians 15. 45–9: Luke 3. 38.
7. Matthew 28. 16.
8. John 10. 16: 11. 51–2: Acts 20. 35.
9. Revelation 21. 21–7.
10. John 10. 14–16: Ephesians 1. 9–10 (NEB): Revelation 21. 23.

Acknowledgements

The author gratefully acknowledges permission to use the following extracts in this book:

Forms of Prayer for Jewish Worship, Oxford University Press, 1977.

Hill, W. D. P. (translator), *Bhagavad-Gita*, Oxford University Press, 1953.

Hume, R. E., *The Thirteen Principal Upanishads*, Oxford University Press, 1931.

Lau, D. C. (translator), *Tao Te Ching*, by Lao Tzu, Penguin Books Ltd., London, 1963.

Mahmud, Abdel Haleem, *The Creed of Islam*, World of Islam Festival Trust, London.

Waley, Arthur, *The Way and the Power*, George Allen & Unwin Ltd., 1934.

— (translator), *Tao Te Ching*, by Lao Tzu, George Allen & Unwin Ltd.

Zaehner, R. C. (translator), *Bhagavad-Gita*, Oxford University Press, 1969.

—, *Hinduism*, Oxford University Press, 1966.

Fount Paperbacks

Fount is one of the leading paperback publishers of religious books and below are some of its recent titles.

- [ ] THE GREAT ACQUITTAL Baker, Carey, Tiller & Wright   £1.50
- [ ] DANCE IN THE DARK Sydney Carter   £1.50
- [ ] THE SACRAMENT OF THE PRESENT MOMENT
      Jean-Pierre de Caussade (trans. Kitty Muggeridge)   £1.25
- [ ] ALL THINGS IN CHRIST Robert Faricy   £2.50 (LF)
- [ ] THE INNER EYE OF LOVE William Johnston   £1.75 (LF)
- [ ] CHRISTIAN REFLECTIONS C. S. Lewis   £1.50
- [ ] PAUL: THE APOSTLE Hugh Montefiore   £1.50
- [ ] GOD'S YES TO SEXUALITY Ed. Rachel Moss   £1.75
- [ ] YOURS FAITHFULLY (Vol. 2) Gerald Priestland   £1.50
- [ ] I BELIEVE HERE AND NOW Rita Snowden   £1.25
- [ ] A GIFT FOR GOD Mother Teresa   £1.00
- [ ] FOUNT CHILDREN'S BIBLE   £3.95 (LF)

All Fount paperbacks are available at your bookshop or news-agent, or they can also be ordered by post from Fount Paperbacks, Cash Sales Department, G.P.O. Box 29, Douglas, Isle of Man, British Isles. Please send purchase price, plus 10p per book. Customers outside the U.K. send purchase price, plus 12p per book. Cheque, postal or money order. No currency.

NAME (Block letters) _____

ADDRESS _____

_____

_____